Haïti
Challenges and Hope

by the Rev. Dr. Jacques E. Pierre

with Study Leader's Guide
by Dr. M. René Johnson

Women's Division · General Board of Global Ministries · The United Methodist Church

Haïti: Challenges & Hope

Copyright © 2011 Women's Division, The General Board of Global Ministries, The United Methodist Church

A publication of the Women's Division, The General Board of Global Ministries, The United Methodist Church

ISBN# 978-1-933663-51-7

Library of Congress Control Number: 2010939380

All photos by Paul Jeffrey, including front- and back-cover images, appear by courtesy of the photographer.

All biblical quotations, unless otherwise noted, are from the New Revised Standard Version (NRSV) of the Bible, copyright © 1989 by the Division of Christian Education of the National Council of Churches of Christ in the United States of America. Used by permission. All rights reserved.

Biblical quotations marked "NIV" are taken from the Holy Bible, NEW INTERNATIONAL VERSION. Copyright © 1973, 1978, 1984 by International Bible Society. All rights reserved throughout the world. Used by permission of International Bible Society.

Biblical quotations marked "KJV" are taken from the King James, or Authorized Version of the Bible.

This book is dedicated to the memory of all of the victims of the January 12, 2010, earthquake, the survivors living in difficult conditions whose energy and faith in God are contagious and inspiring, all those from around the world who are earnestly laboring to alleviate the suffering of the population, all the lay- and clergypersons in The Methodist Church in Haïti proclaiming the Good News of the kingdom of God and all those working daily for economic and social justice to become a reality in Haïti.

A woman carries produce to sell in the market in the Bel-Air neighborhood of Port-au-Prince, Haïti. *(Paul Jeffrey)*

A ruined market in Port-au-Prince, Haïti, which was rocked by a devastating earthquake on January 12, 2010. *(Paul Jeffrey)*

Table of Contents

Acknowledgments 3

Introduction 5

Selected Timeline of Key Events in Haïti 7

Chapter 1: The Land and Its People 13
    Geographic Location of Haïti 13
    Name Changes Throughout History 13
    The People Who Populated the Land of Haïti 14
    Haïtian Culture 17
    Overview of Haïti's Socioeconomic Structure 20

Chapter 2: Toward a Haïtian Liberation Theology 23
    Rationale for a Haïtian Liberation Theology 24
    Origin of the Theology of Liberation 26
    Brief History of Christianity in Haïti 27
    Developing a Haïtian Liberation Theology for Today 28
    Conclusion 33

Chapter 3: Gone in 35 Seconds: The 35 Seconds That Changed Haïti's Landscape 37
    The Scope of the Devastation 38
    The People's Solidarity 39

Chapter 4: Links of Solidarity and Partnership 45
    Ongoing Relationship Between The United Methodist Church
        and The Methodist Church in Haïti 46
    The Haïti–Michigan Covenant 48
    The Haïti–Florida Covenant 49
    Avenues for Partnership With Haïti 50

Chapter 5: Challenges and Opportunities for Haïti and Its People 53
    Haïti's Challenges Prior to the January 12 Earthquake 53
    Summary of New Challenges Brought by the Earthquake 54
    New Opportunities for Haïti and Its People 55

Epilogue: Hopes and Dreams for Haïti and Its People. 59

Bibliography 65

Study Leader's Guide 69
        Single-session Option (One Hour) 73
        Four-session Option (Two-hour Sessions) 77
        Session 1: The Legacy of History and Culture 77
        Session 2: The Role of Faith in Social Justice 82
        Session 3: Preaching a Vision of Hope 89
        Session 4: Putting Love in Action 92

Appendixes 99
        Appendix A: The Clinton Foundation Press Release 99
        Appendix B: Haïti Response Project Overview 100
        Appendix C: Haïtian Artisans for Peace International 103
        Appendix D: Haïti–Michigan Covenant 109
        Appendix E: Haïti–Florida Covenant 112
        Appendix F: The Institute of Preaching 114
        Appendix G: Groups Begin Preliminary Work for Long-term Recovery in Haïti 116
        Appendix H: Memoir of Haïti 118

Deeper Meaning of the Haïtian Proverbs 119

About the Authors 121

Acknowledgments

> *Bay piti pa chich*
> (Give little isn't greedy)
>
> *Di mèsi jwenn ankò*
> (Say thank-you receive again)

I am indebted to so many people who assisted me and shared their insights and knowledge with me in the preparation of this study that I am almost certain I forgot to mention some of them by name. To those, I sincerely apologize and want them to know that I am grateful for their generous assistance.

I would like, particularly, to acknowledge the contribution of my brothers and sisters in Haïti who warned me about some of the pitfalls in which so many writers about Haïti had fallen and steered me in the right direction. I am deeply grateful to the Rev. Gesner Paul, President of The Methodist Church in Haïti[1], and to my friend Edzaire Paul, director of the Bureau de l'Église Méthodiste Haïti pour l'Éducation Générale (Office of The Methodist Church in Haïti for Education) BEHMEG, who, in spite of their busy schedules found time to meet with me and share valuable information and insights that I used in this book. I am also indebted to Jean Paul William, a former colleague at the (COD) Bureau de Coordination de l'Église Méthodiste (Co-ordination Bureau of The Methodist Church in Haïti), an adult educator and a community organizer whose commitment to the masses of Haïti remains unwavering even in the face of the greatest challenges he has seen in his life and career. I thank the Rev. Jean Jacques Ralph Denizard, superintendent of the Circuits of Petit-Goâve and La Gonâve of The Methodist Church in Haïti, and his wife Joanne, who welcomed me into their home and guided me in the cities of Petit-Goâve and Port-au-Prince during my trips to Haïti to collect data.

My sincere thanks to my wife, the Rev. M. Pascale Délisma-Pierre, who encouraged me to accept the challenge to write this book. In spite of her multiple obligations as a full-time educator, doctoral student and co-pastor of a new congregation, Pascale found time to read the manuscript and ask pertinent questions. She also contributed in writing the chapter on Haïtian culture. Without her encouragements and participation, this mission study would not have been possible. I am also grateful to my sister, Judith Pierre-Okerson, who proposed that I be the writer of the study on Haïti.

I am grateful to the members of the reviewing team who read the drafts of this study and made suggestions and recommendations to improve the document.

I am indebted to the Rev. Dr. Leslie Griffiths, author of *History of Methodism in Haïti*, whose book was the primary source I utilized for the early period of Methodism in Haïti. Dr. Griffiths is a Welshman from the British Methodist Church who served as a Methodist minister in Haïti for more than 10 years.

Notes

1. The official name of the church is The Methodist Church in Haïti, translated in French as L'Église Méthodiste d'Haïti (EMH). It is one of the eight district conferences of The Methodist Church in the Caribbean and the Americas (MCCA), whose connectional conference office is in Belmont, St. John's, Antigua, W.I. The district conferences of the MCCA are Haïti, Jamaica, Guyana, Bahamas/Turk and Caicos, Panama/Costa Rica, Leeward Island, Belize/Honduras and the South Caribbean Islands. Although it is sometimes called The Methodist Church of Haïti, The Methodist Church in Haïti is not the official church of Haïti.

Introduction

> *Pale mal se lapriyè jouda*
> (Speaking evil is gossipers' prayer)
>
> *Se sou chen mèg sèlman yo wè pis*
> (They see fleas only on skinny dogs)

Haïti is the site of the first and only successful slave revolution in the world and the second independent nation in the Americas after the United States. The timing and the circumstances in which Haïti earned its freedom have made this country the target of much aggression and slander from the world powers throughout its more than two centuries of history. Haïti declared its independence from France on January 1, 1804. At that time, slavery and colonialism were at their height in the Western world. These example" from spreading throughout the Caribbean, Latin America and the United States. Consequently, since its independence, Haïti has been the unfortunate recipient of numerous aggressions and constant calumnies from most of the world.

For many decades, Haïti has been portrayed around the world in feature films, documentaries, television programs, news articles and books, as well as in countless reports of nongovernmental organizations

> **"Haïti is the site of the first and only successful slave revolution in the world and the second independent nation in the Americas after the United States."**

ploitation systems were sources of wealth and bragging rights for slave-holding and colonial powers, such as France, England, Spain, Portugal and the United States.

The African men and women who liberated Haïti did not win their freedom through negotiation and consensus but by fighting with all their soul and with all their strength to overcome one of the most cruel and powerful forces of the time: Napoleon Bonaparte's French army. This defeat offended not only the French but also the other slave-holding and colonial powers. They wanted, at all costs, to crush the former slaves and their newly established independent nation. Their aim was to choke Haïti from the start to prevent its "bad (NGOs) as a backward country of poor and illiterate people who cannot govern themselves. It is rare to hear the name of Haïti mentioned without one of these statements or phrases preceding or following it: the poorest country in the Western Hemisphere, a country marked by political violence and social unrest, boat people, drug trafficking, dictatorship, Vodou[1] and so forth. To illustrate these views, there are always pictures of a starving child, an older woman or a pregnant woman carrying wood or groceries home from a local market, a street protest or an uncollected trash pile in a slum. Although some of these statements and phrases about Haïti have some truth, none of them gives a full picture of the country. Some people who have visited

Haïti only a few times and learned the Haïtian greeting "*Sak pase?*" "*Nap boule*" ("What's up?" "Fine.") assume they are "experts" on Haïti and are ready to explain to others the complicated religious, social, cultural, economic and political realities of the country. As a result, they often spread erroneous or biased ideas about Haïti.

This study on Haïti does not assume it captures every aspect of Haïti and its people's daily realities, their rich and vivacious culture or their long history of struggles and ingenuities. Reading this book will definitely not make anyone an "expert" on Haïti. While providing the reader with a glimpse into the history, geography, culture and the religious life of Haïti, this book limits itself to exploring the current challenges the people of Haïti and The Methodist Church in Haïti are facing.

The primary purpose of this endeavor is to encourage ongoing exchanges of cultural understanding, mutual respect and mission partnership between the people of The United Methodist Church and the people of God in Haïti. This study also explores the links of solidarity and partnership between The United Methodist Church and The Methodist Church in Haïti. It is an open invitation to everyone everywhere seeking a partnership with non-governmental organizations to assist the Haïtian people in facing their current challenges to create a better future.

Notes

1. *Vodou* is the proper spelling of the Americanized word "voodoo." It is a religion with origins in Africa that is very popular in Haïti. Vodou is also practiced in the West Indies and in the southern United States. For the purpose of the study on Haïti, the Haïtian spelling is used throughout this book.

A woman cooks in front of her home in the Haïtian village of Vaudreuil. She used a small loan to buy what she needed to start the business, in which she sells cooked food to her neighbors who have money to spend. *(Paul Jeffrey)*

Selected Timeline of Key Events in Haïti

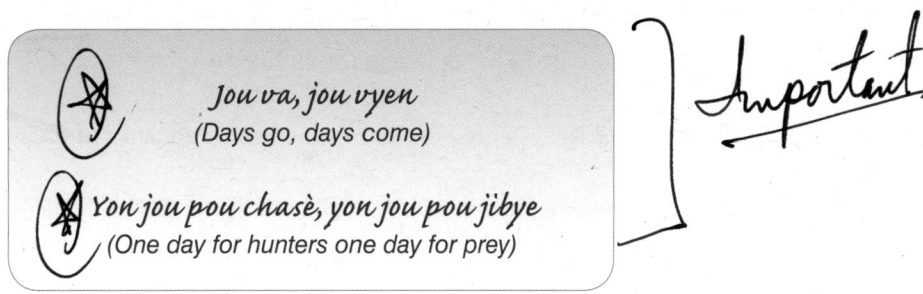

1492	Christopher Columbus lands in the island that the Arawaks, the indigenous people, call *Haïti*, which means "mountainous land"; Columbus names the new land *Hispaniola* (Little Spain), then renames it *Santo Domingo*.
1496	The Spanish establish a permanent settlement in Santo Domingo, now the capital of the Dominican Republic.
1503	The first African slaves arrive in Santo Domingo to replace the Arawaks, who are exploited and massacred by the Spanish.
1697	Spain cedes the western part of Hispaniola, now the Republic of Haïti, to France; France names its territory Saint Domingue.
1779	France authorizes about 750 African fighters, free men from Haïti to join the American and French troops to fight against British soldiers in Savannah, Georgia, for American independence (General Henri Christophe, the first king of northern Haïti, is among the freedom fighters).
1791	A massive slave revolt begins with a religious Vodou ceremony led by Boukman, a Maroon (runaway slave) and Vodou priest from Jamaica.
1801	A former slave, Toussaint Louverture, successfully leads a slave revolution, liberates Hispaniola, unifies the island into one territory and abolishes slavery.
1801	The first constitution is published in Saint Domingue without the approval of the French authorities; Louverture is given the title of general-governor for life.

1802	French forces led by Napoleon Bonaparte's brother-in-law, General Charles Leclerc, are defeated by the indigenous army led by Toussaint Louverture.
1802	Louverture, betrayed by his colleagues, is arrested and deported to France where he dies in prison.
1803	Former slave Jean-Jacques Dessalines, leader of the revolutionary army, publishes the Independence Decree in Gonaives and vows with his generals "to live free or die."
1804	Haïti becomes the first independent black nation in the world, and Dessalines is crowned Emperor of Haïti.
1806	Dessalines is assassinated in Port-au-Prince and Haïti is divided into two countries, a black-led kingdom in the north led by Henri Christophe and a Mulatto-led republic in the south headed by Alexandre Pétion.
1807	The Senate impeaches Christophe, and Pétion is elected president of Haïti.
1816	Fleeing from the Spanish Army, Simón Bolívar, the liberator of Latin America, meets with Pétion in Port-au-Prince; Pétion gives weapons, money and food to Bolívar and allows him to recruit Haïtians to join him in the fight for freedom; Pétion requests that Bolívar free all slaves in the countries he will liberate.
1818	Pétion dies of natural causes, and his personal secretary, Jean-Pierre Boyer, is elected president for life. Boyer governs Haïti for 25 years and the entire island for 21 years.
1842	A violent earthquake shakes the entire island, causes serious damage and destroys the city of Cap Haïtian.
1915	Under the pretext of social and economic instabilities, the United States invades Haïti and assumes control of the country's finances and natural resources.
1934	The United States withdraws its troops from Haïti but maintains fiscal control of the country until 1941.
1957	Dr. François Duvalier, "Papa Doc," is elected president for a six-year term.

1958	Duvalier forms the paramilitary group Volontaires de la Sécurité Nationale (Volunteers for the National Security or VSN) known as the Tonton Macoutes (the Bogeymen).
1962	In controversial elections, Duvalier is re-elected for another six-year term.
1964	Duvalier amends the constitution, declares himself president for life and establishes a dictatorship with the help of the military and the Tonton Macoutes.
1970	Duvalier amends the constitution to lower the minimum age to be president from 35 to 18 years.
1971	Duvalier dies of natural causes and is succeeded by his 19-year-old son, Jean-Claude Duvalier, known as "Baby Doc."
1980	Creole becomes an official language in Haïti in addition to French.
1986	Jean-Claude Duvalier flees from Haïti in the wake of mounting popular discontent and is replaced by a governing council, Le Conseil National de Gouvernement (the National Council of Government), led by Lieutenant-General Henri Namphy.
1986	Namphy dissolves the paramilitary group VSN and discretely offers protection to its leaders at the presidential palace.
1987	A new constitution that bans the members of the Tonton Macoutes from seeking elected offices is approved by the Haïtian people.
1987	The first free elections in decades are aborted in a bloodshed orchestrated by the military to hold on to power.
1988	Dr. Leslie François Manigat becomes president on February 7 in the fraudulent elections organized by the military and is ousted June 20 by a military coup led by Brigadier General Prosper Avril.
1989	Avril is overthrown by a military uprising, and Lieutenant General Herard Abraham takes control of the presidency for 48 hours. Herta Pascal-Trouillot is installed as the first female president of Haïti until the general elections take place.
1990	Jean-Bertrand Aristide, a former Catholic priest and a popular activist, is elected president for five years.

A woman winnows corn in the Haïtian village of Foret des Pins. *(Paul Jeffrey)*

1990	During Pascal-Trouillot's interim government, Dr. Roger Lafontant, a former member of Jean-Claude Duvalier's government and one of the national leaders of the Tonton Macoutes, attempts to seize power in a coup d'état with the alleged support of the American Embassy in Haïti; Lafontant is later assassinated in his jail cell.
1991	Aristide is inaugurated president of Haïti for five years under the new constitution.
1991	Aristide is ousted in a military coup led by Brigadier General Raoul Cedras, triggering sanctions by the United States and the Organization of American States.
1991–1992	Several thousands of Haïtians risk their lives at sea to flee the brutal repression from the military and their paramilitary allies. Captured by the U.S. Coast Guard, the refugees are detained and processed in Guantanamo Bay, Cuba. The majority of them, including unaccompanied minors, are returned to Haïti, and around 11,000 of the refugees are transferred into the United States to seek asylum.
1993	Le Front pour l'Avancement et le Progrès d'Haïti (The Front for the Advancement and Progress of Haïti) FRAPH, an anti-Aristide paramilitary group led by CIA informant Emmanuel "ToTo" Constant, terrorizes the population with impunity until the return of Aristide in 1994.
1993	The United Nations imposes stronger sanctions against Haïti after the military regime rejects an accord facilitating Aristide's return to power.

1994	The military regime relinquishes power in the face of an imminent U.S. invasion. U.S. forces oversee a transition to a civilian government. U.S. President Bill Clinton returns Aristide to power and Aristide dissolves the Haïtian army.
1995	United Nations peacekeepers begin to replace the U.S. troops. Aristide's supporters win parliamentary elections. René Garcia Préval, Aristide's former prime minister, is elected president to replace Aristide.
1999	Following a series of disagreements with deputies, Préval declares the parliament term has expired and begins ruling by decree.
2000	Aristide is elected president for a second term (nonconsecutive) amid allegations of irregularities.
2001	Armed militia connected to some of the former officers in the army attack some police stations and kill four police officers. Thirty armed men attempt to seize the National Palace.
2002	Haïti is approved as a full member of the Caribbean Community (CARICUM) trade block.
2003	Aristide recognizes Vodou as a religion in Haïti and gives to its adherents the same civil and religious privileges as Catholics and Protestants.
2004	The U.S. government overthrows Aristide and forces him into exile; an interim government led by François Latortue is installed.
2006	Préval is elected president a second time (nonconsecutive term) and launches a campaign to disarm gang members in exchange for job training.
2008	Préval's government announces an emergency plan to cut prices in an attempt to halt social unrest. The United States and the World Bank announce extra food aid to Haïti totaling $30 million.
2009	Former U.S. President Clinton is appointed United Nations special envoy to Haïti.
2009	The World Bank and the International Monetary Fund cancel $1.2 billion of Haïti's debt (80 percent of the total) after judging it to have fulfilled economic reform and poverty reduction conditions.
2010	Over 300,000 people are killed when a magnitude 7.0 earthquake hits the capital, Port-au-Prince, and its wider region—the worst natural disaster in Haïti since 1842.

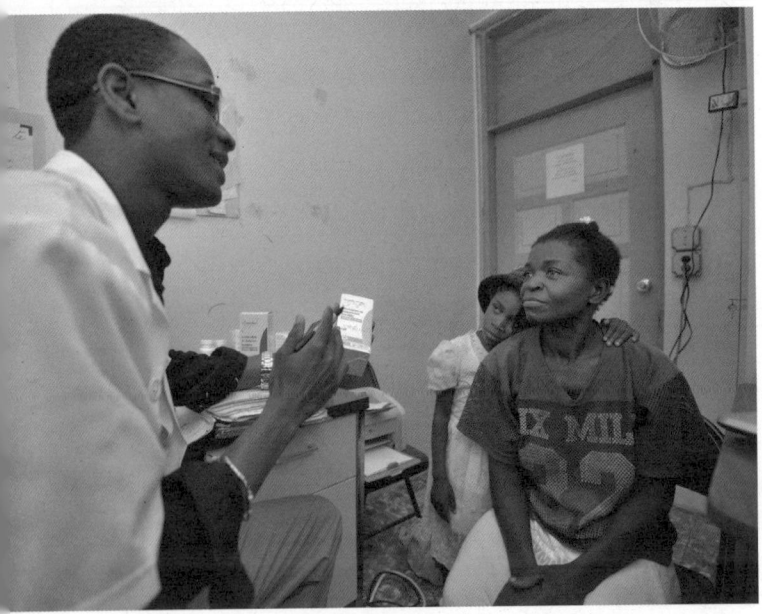

(left side) A woman carries bananas to sell in the Croix-des-Bossales market in the La Saline neighborhood of Port-au-Prince, Haïti; pharmacist Jean Darcelin explains the dosage on antiretroviral medication to Matilde Meleus, at the St Boniface Hospital in Fond des Blancs, Haïti, while her 6-year old daughter Ketia looks on.

(right side) Two girls walk to school in the Haïtian village of Foret des Pins; children on the way home from school in the Haïtian village of Foret des Pins; a woman plants beans in her field outside the village of Mare Rouge in Haiti's poverty-stricken northwest. *(all images Paul Jeffrey)*

Chapter One
The Land and Its People

> *Dèyè mòn gen mòn*
> (Behind a mountain there is another mountain)

The island of which the Republic of Haïti is a part has endured many name changes to suit its rulers throughout its long history. However, the indigenous name has survived, at least in the western part of the island. This chapter locates Haïti vis-à-vis its Caribbean neighbors and traces the different name changes. It also provides some snapshots of the people who populated this land and an overview of Haïti's cultural heritage as well as of its socioeconomic structures.

Geographic Location of Haïti

The island of Haïti, also known as *Hispaniola*, is, after Cuba, the second largest landmass in the Greater Antilles. Covering an area of about 78,250 square kilometers, it is surrounded by the Atlantic Ocean and the Caribbean Sea. Contrary to some people's assumption, the name *Haïti* was given not only to the territory occupied by the Republic of Haïti but also to the entire island that is shared by the Republic of Haïti and the Dominican Republic. The Republic of Haïti occupies the western part of the island, about one-third, and the Dominican Republic has the eastern side, about two-thirds of the island. The Republic of Haïti is located between Cuba to the northwest, Jamaica to the southwest and the Dominican Republic to the east. Haïti is a short 90-minute flight from Miami, Florida. With 27,700 square kilometers, it is about the size of the state of Maryland.

Name Changes Throughout History

> *Gen pouvwa nan non*
> (There is power in names)

The name *Haïti* comes from the language of the Arawaks, the indigenous inhabitants of the land. It means "high land" or "mountainous land." Ignorant of the name of the island, when Christopher Columbus and the Spanish explorers landed in Haïti in 1492, they called it *Hispaniola*. Later, they renamed the island *Santo Domingo* (Saint Sunday) to commemorate the day they landed in this part of the New World.

In 1697, Spain ceded the western part of the island to France and kept the eastern side, which became the Dominican Republic. In French, the name translated as *Saint Domingue*. On December 31, 1803, former slave Jean-Jacques Dessalines, leader of the revolutionary army, gathered with his generals in the city of Gonaïves to read the Independence Decree. Capturing this moment, the historian J. C. Dorsainvil asserted, "Dessalines wanted to celebrate the independence proclamation in a solemn ceremony. To show his desire to

The Niña, Pinta and Santa Maria, an engraving circa 1882. *(istockphoto.com/ Constance McGuire)*

forget completely France and the colonial and slavery systems, he gave back to Saint Domingue its indigenous name, *Haïti*."[1] On January 1, 1804, Saint Domingue officially ceased to exist, and Haïti was reborn as the first independent black nation in the new world.

The People Who Populated the Land of Haïti

To understand the Haïtian culture, it is paramount to know about the people who populated this land throughout its history and whose customs and cultural values have intersected directly or indirectly through the years. The overwhelming majority of people living on the American continents are not indigenous to that part of the world. At some point in history, their ancestors voluntarily or involuntarily migrated to America from Europe, Africa or Asia. In the case of Haïti, the land was populated by the Arawaks and the Caribs (from which the word *Caribbean* comes) before Christopher Columbus and his explorers were lost on their voyage to India and landed there.

The Indigenous People of Haïti

Although a small group of Caribs shared life on the island, the Arawaks were the larger population of Haïti. Compared to the peaceful and hospitable manners of the latter, the Caribs were warriors, who attacked their neighbors to expand their hunting grounds and find mates. However, contrary to popular colonial propaganda and the predominant European views, the indigenous people were not savages. They were highly organized and politically structured as five tribes or *caciques*, each considered a separate kingdom. The Arawaks were polytheistic and very religious. Their gods and the focus of their worship ceremonies were

> "The indigenous people were not savages. They were highly organized and politically structured as five tribes or *caciques*, each considered a separate kingdom."

nature-oriented. Archeologists have found in Haïti many stones and other religious artifacts that suggest the Arawaks believed in an afterlife. They estimate the population of the Arawaks at between 400,000 and 4,000,000 people prior to the Spanish colonization.

Due to harsh and inhumane treatment from the Spanish and the diseases they brought to the island, by 1507 the population of the Arawaks had shrunk to 60,000. Twenty-four years later, in 1531, their numbers dwin-

African Slaves Boiling Sugarcane. Steel engraving from 1882.
(istockphoto.com/Graffissimo)

dled to 600 people. Today, traces of the Arawaks are scarcely visible in Haïti. The use of the canoe for fishing and short-distance water transportation, the making of cassava[2] and the consumption of foods such as yams, yucca and corn are among the rare evidence of the Arawaks cultural heritage that has survived in Haïti.

> **"In addition to their weapons and greed, the Spanish also brought their religion, Christianity, to the new world."**

The Spanish Presence
Two months after landing in San Salvador on October 12, 1492, Christopher Columbus and his crew arrived in Haïti on Sunday, December 5, 1492. They built their first settlement in Môle Saint Nicolas, in the northwestern coast of the Republic of Haïti. In spite of the hospitable welcome and the assistance in food that the Arawaks gave to the Spanish explorers, the Europeans did not reciprocate with kindness. They committed genocide against the Arawaks and remained the sole rulers of the entire island until 1697.

In addition to their weapons and greed, the Spanish also brought their religion, Christianity, to the new world. Prior to their departure from Spain, the conquistadors received a mandate from the pope to convert to Christianity the people of the lands that they would conquer. Thus, Catholic priests accompanied the sailors. The indigenous people were subjected to Catholicism and the Spanish missionaries prohibited many of their religious artifacts and customs, which the Spanish considered idolatrous.

The Arawaks's religious symbols and jewelry made of gold or silver were seized, melted and shipped to Spain. The Spanish also brought their language, music, attire and the art of writing to the island.

The African Presence
The presence of African slaves in colonial America was first recorded in 1619. However, Africans already had been living in bondage in Hispaniola under Spanish rule for more than 100 years. Alarmed by the rapid decrease of the native population and determined to exploit the rich soil of the mountainous land, the Spanish looked to Africa to replace the Arawaks as forced laborers. In 1503, under the government of Nicolas Ovando, the first group of Africans was brought to Santo Domingo to work as slaves, mostly in the mines. The savagery of the Europeans was not limited to the Arawaks; they treated the Africans with as much cruelty.

When they arrived in Santo Domingo, the Africans were also forced to adopt Christianity. They never abandoned their own religious beliefs, however, even though the practice of their religion was outlawed. The first Africans who were brought to the New World were either kidnapped or purchased by European slave traders from the African coastal lands of Togo, Benin, Ghana, Ivory Coast and Liberia. They were heterogeneous groups with many different cultural heritages.

Similar to the Arawaks of Haïti, the West Africans were polytheistic. They believed there was a high god who created all things and many lesser gods who were subject to the high god. In addition to the high god, the Africans worshiped and prayed to specific lesser gods for particular needs, such as rain, harvest, fertility, protection and so forth. They also believed that the spirits of their ancestors occupied a status with the lesser gods. These kinds of beliefs are still pervasive in Haïtian Vodou.

The French Presence

The first French subjects who landed in Santo Domingo were pirates seeking to make their fortunes by attacking the Spanish ships transporting goods in and out of the island. These adventurers first arrived in 1625 and established themselves on the island of La Tortue, on the northwestern coast of today's Haïti. The French translated the Spanish Santo Domingo as Saint Domingue, a name that remained until Haïti's independence in 1804. The French pirates progressively moved inland and captured several cities from the Spanish. The armed struggles between the French and the Spanish for the control of the island continued until 1697, when these two European powers participated in the signing of the Ryswick Treaty. This accord settled the War of the Grand Alliance in which France opposed the League

> **After repeated victories of the revolutionary army, the leaders of the slaves declared their independence from France on January 1, 1804.**

of Augsburg (Spain, England, the Holy Roman Empire and the United Provinces). As a part of the Treaty of Ryswick, signed on September 20, 1697, Spain ceded the western third of the island, which became Haïti, to France. The French remained rulers of this territory almost unchallenged until 1789. On August 29 of that year, the African slaves began their long, armed struggle against slavery in Saint Domingue.

After repeated victories of the revolutionary army, the leaders of the slaves declared their independence from France on January 1, 1804. Following this event, most of the French who were living in Saint Domingue were either deported to France or killed. Yet the French's cultural heritage remained one of the strongest in the Haïtian sociocultural landscape until recently. In addition to the French language, the French colonialists left their education and class systems in Haïti.

The U.S. Presence

After the colonial powers of Europe, Spain and France made their fortunes in Haïti, it was time for the United States, a rising power at the time, to tap into Haïti's

Local artisans have painted colorful murals outside a school in Mizak, a remote Haïtian village.
(Paul Jeffrey)

resources. In 1915, Haïti had once again experienced a social and political crisis that led to violence and political unrest. On August 12, 1915, the United States of America invaded Haïti. The U.S. military ruled Haïti with an iron fist for 19 years and crushed all opposition to their presence with horrific violence that exceeded the violence they used as a pretext to invade the country.

> **The U.S. military ruled Haïti with an iron fist for 19 years and crushed all opposition to their presence with horrific violence that exceeded the violence they used as a pretext to invade the country.**

Charlemagne Péralte, the leader of the freedom fighters named the "Cacos," vehemently opposed Sud Dartiguenave, who was installed as president by the U.S. military. Péralte rallied support throughout the country for a new independence movement to end the U.S. occupation. On November 1, 1919, Charlemagne Péralte was betrayed, trapped and killed by the U.S. Marines. His naked body was tied to a door and left in public display as an intimidating example to other Cacos.

Many of Péralte's companions were also brutally massacred; about 3,000 were killed. In spite of the harsh treatment and repression by the U.S. military, the Haïtian citizens continued to fight against the occupation of their country. After repeated protests, the United States withdrew its troops from Haïti in 1934. Nevertheless, the U.S. authorities continued to control the financial resources of Haïti until 1941, seven years after the occupation officially ended. They also left the "gendarmerie," which later became the Haïtian army, as an instrument of repression against the people and a tool to perpetuate U.S. influence on Haïti's political affairs.

Through interaction with the Haïtian population, some North American language infiltrated and blended into Haïtian Creole, the more widely spoken of the two languages in Haïti. North American influence on Haïti was not limited to the economic, political and linguistic realms; it also touched the religious life of the country. Many of the Protestant denominations that are currently operating in Haïti came to the country after the U.S. occupation.

Haïtian Culture

The Haïtian culture is a symbiosis of West Indian, Spanish, French, North American and African traditions and customs. The official languages of Haïti are French and Haïtian Creole. The latter is more prominent and is widely utilized in music, religious ceremonies, literature and drama.

All Haïtians speak Creole, whereas only about 20 percent of the population is fluent in French. Until the 1990s, Creole was the language of everyday conversation and life while French was the medium of education and the official business of the government.

Haïti: Challenges and Hope | 17

As his family sings along, a man plays his guitar at the end of a day in the Haïtian village of Foret des Pins.
(Paul Jeffrey)

Haïtians are extremely creative and artistic. The unique features and colorful portrayal in their art works earn worldwide appreciation. In addition to arts and crafts, music constitutes a major part of the Haïtian culture.

Haïtian Music

> *Depi tanbou frape fòk Ayisyen danse*
> (Whenever the drum beats,
> Haitians have to dance)

Haïtian music is influenced by African, French, Spanish and American rhythms. The drum is widely used in Haïtian songs and dances. The most popular musical style in Haïti is *Compas* (pronounced "kunpa"). It is a musical rhythm that has the flair of Merengue. In addition to Compas, Haïtians also enjoy *Rara*, a popular street music played during the Easter season; *Rasin*, an African rhythm played in Vodou ceremonies; and Haïtian rap. Haïtian music is also influenced by American jazz, Caribbean calypso, Reggae, hip-hop and French ballades.

The biggest music festival in Haïti is the yearly Carnival. It takes place in the month of February and lasts three days. During this festivity, floats of musical groups and dancers parade nonstop on the Carnival routes. The Haïtian Carnival is a national event of extravagant proportion. It is a mixture of color, beauty, food, music, dance and lively street parties. During this period, barriers erected by social classes and economic status are broken and people escape from their daily routines and descend on the streets singing, dancing and rejoicing together.

18 | Chapter 1

> "**Vodou is not only about casting spells on people. Its adherents rely on their priests for healing and counseling in many areas of their lives.**"

Religion in Haïti

Bondye bon; Bondye pi fò
(God is good; God is omnipotent)

In addition to lively music, dance and colorful artworks, religion plays a significant role in the life of the Haïtian people. The primary religions practiced in Haïti are Christianity and Vodou. The latter is the religion the Africans brought with them to the "new world." The word *Vodou* came from the Fon word *Voudon*, which means "the power that is invisible." Although Vodou teaches belief in the highest god, the creator of all things, it also encourages beliefs in, and the invocation of, many lesser gods called *loas*.

In Haïti, images of Catholic saints represent most of the loas, in part because the slaves had to hide their gods in the images of the catholic saints in order to worship and make offerings to them. For instance, Saint James represents the loa "Ogu Feray," and the image of the Virgin Mary represents the loa "Ezili Freda." Contrary to the depictions of its detractors, Vodou is not only about casting spells on people. Its adherents rely on their priests for healing and counseling in many areas of their lives.

In the rural areas, Vodou priests are often consulted as medicine men and women. Vodou also has many moral teachings similar to those found in Christianity. Vodou is also about joyful worship of the gods and the celebration of the ancestors' spirits, the loas, who are in communion with the worshipers and constantly watch over them. In spite of prohibition and repression in colonial times and persecution and slander in later years, Vodou has survived and is still strong in Haïti's religious landscape.

Catholicism, the first branch of Christianity established in the country, came with the Spanish and continued with the French colonizers. Even after the independence of Haïti, Roman Catholicism continued to dominate Haïtian religious life. Two articles of the 1811 Constitution of the Republic of Haïti confirm this fact: Article 48, "Roman Catholic Church, being for all Haïtians, is the national church and its clergy are protected," and Article 50, "The President, in consultation with the Pope, chooses a bishop to further young Haïtian priests."[3]

Symbol of Papa Legba, the Haïtian Vodou god who acts as an intermediary between the loa and humans. He is also the god of the crossroads; he opens the road to the spirit world. *(istockphoto.com/james74)*

Haïti: Challenges and Hope | 19

> **"In 1817, the first Methodist missionaries, John Brown and James Catts, two laymen, arrived in Port-au-Prince from the British colony of Saint Thomas. This was the first official Protestant presence in the country."**

Although early Haïtian laws gave preference to the Roman Catholic Church, they did not prohibit the existence of Protestantism. In its 49th article, the 1811 Constitution stipulated, "Any other cult is permitted as long as it obeys the laws." Sir Francis Reynalds, captain of the ship *Hébé* and a Methodist layman, took advantage of this provision for religious diversity in 1815. During his only voyage to Haïti, he wrote to President Alexandre Pétion to request permission to establish a Methodist mission in Haïti.[4] To his great satisfaction, the president granted Reynalds's petition two days before he left Haïti. Two years later, in 1817, the first Methodist missionaries to Haïti, John Brown and James Catts, two laymen, arrived in Port-au-Prince from the British colony of Saint Thomas. This was the first official Protestant presence in the country.

In addition to Methodism, several other denominations have established churches in Haïti. The Episcopalians and the Baptists came in 1861, followed by the Adventists in 1879. The American occupation of Haïti helped Protestantism develop further in the country. Denominations such as the Assemblies of God (in 1945), the Nazarene Church (in 1948), the Salvation Army (in 1950), the Pentecostal Church (in 1962) and the Church of God (in 1969) came to Haïti after the occupation. The first Lutheran church in Haïti was founded in 1980. Author Jules Casséus notes, "By 1980, Haïti had more than 200 different missions or denominations."[5]

Finding reliable statistical information about religions in Haïti is a daunting task. The only clear line of division that exists is between Catholics and Protestants. The latter represent about 35 percent of the population. Although Vodou has been a recognized religion in Haïti since 2003 and more than 70 percent of Haïtians' lives are permeated one way or another by Vodou beliefs, the Catholic Church claims 65.3 percent of the population. The reason for this discrepancy may be because almost all of the Vodou adherents were baptized in the Catholic Church. Although many of these people may never attend a Catholic mass, except for an occasional wedding or funeral, the church counts all of them among its members, even those who do not think of themselves as Christians.

Overview of Haïti's Socioeconomic Structure

One of France's legacies to Haïti is the class system. During French colonization, Saint Domingue had three distinct socioeconomic classes: "Les Blancs," (white people), the "Affranchis" (the freedmen) and slaves. Les Blancs possessed all of the financial resources and had all of the civil and political rights in the society. The Affranchis were mostly Mulattos (half black and half white), the sons and daughters of a white man and of a black or Mulatto woman. (While *mulatto* is sometimes used as a term of derision in North America, Mulattos are a recognized people group in Haïti and throughout Latin America.) In rare cases, there were a few freed black people among the Affranchis. This group had limited financial privileges through paid work for Les Blancs, but they did not have civil or political rights. At the bottom of the society were the slaves. They were the engine of the colony's economic activities and impressive wealth yet they did not receive any benefit from their hard labor and did not have any rights. In fact, slaves were considered not as human beings but as properties to be sold, donated, traded or inherited. During the colonial era, 87 percent of the population was African slaves, 8 percent whites and 5 percent freedmen. Although the representatives of the colonial class system disappeared after independence, forms of the class system continue to exist in Haïti.

With the success of the 1804 slave revolution and the subsequent independence of the new nation, the structure of the class system was dismantled. Most of the white owners of the plantations and of the agro-industries were either killed or repatriated to France. Many of the former slaves became military leaders, officers and soldiers in the army. Some plantations were destroyed and others subdivided and distributed among the officers and soldiers. This process gave birth to two distinct groups. On the one hand were the military leaders and the urban elites; on the other, the peasants and soldiers. The urban elites were overwhelmingly the educated and wealthy Mulattos who occupied high positions in the government and in the trade industry.

The Mulattos used their alliance with the military leaders, whom they used as an instrument to maintain and increase their hegemony over the economy and politics of the country for many generations. Starting in the 1950s, however, with the ascension to the presidency of Dumarsais Estimé and François Duvalier, a thin but growing black middle class began to appear. Although there are several layers inside each one of these groups, mirrored from the colonial era, Haïti still has three basic socioeconomic classes: the upper class (the very rich), the middle class and the masses.

In the 1980s, Haïti's upper class, made primarily of Mulattos and heirs of the German, English, Danish and Arabs who migrated to the country in the early 1900s, constituted as little as 2 percent of the total population. Nevertheless, they controlled about 44 percent of the national resources. The middle class, about 5 percent of the population, counted among its members military leaders, educated blacks working for the government and Mulattos working for the upper class. The masses, representing the overwhelming majority of the population (more than 90 percent), was composed of the peasants living in the countryside and those who migrated to the slums in Port-au-Prince and other major cities.

Today, Haïti's middle class has increased considerably, but a few families of the upper class continue to dominate the country's economy. While this group gets richer and richer, the masses become more and more destitute.[6]

Notes

1. J. C. Dorsainvil, *Histoire d'Haïti* (Port-au-Prince, Haïti: Edition Henri Deschamps, 1942), 115.
2. Cassava is a fibrous tuber, often made into flatbread and cooked over an open fire.
3. Leslie J. Griffiths. *A History of Methodism in Haïti* (Port-au-Prince, Haïti: Imprimerie Methodist DEL, 1986), 17.
4. Ibid., 13.
5. Jules Casséus, *Haïti: Quelle Église . . . Quelle Liberation? (Haïti: What Church . . . What Liberation?)* (Miami, Fla.: The Little River Press, 1991).
6. While former President Jean Bertrand Aristide is a significant figure in the history of Haïti, he is also extremely polarizing. Regardless of what one says about him, it is likely to start a heated controversy (for not saying enough or for saying too much). I have referred, therefore, to the socioeconomic shifts and conditions in modern-day Haïti rather than to the individuals who lead or may be identified with those shifts.

A man holds a crucifix and candle during a mass in the shadows of the ruins of the Roman Catholic Cathedral of Our Lady of the Assumption in Port-au-Prince, Haïti, devastated in the January 12, 2010, earthquake. *(Paul Jeffrey)*

Chapter Two
Toward a Haïtian Liberation Theology

> *Bondye gen kè sansib pou pòv yo*
> (God's heart is compassionate
> toward the poor)

The topic for this chapter came from the many discussions and reflections I had as a young lay preacher in The Methodist Church in Haïti with the late J. Wildès Joseph, a fellow lay preacher and adult educator.

Life in the context of oppression and exploitation of the poor and corruption in the government and the churches gave liberation theologies and transformative education a place of choice in our hearts, our daily conversations, our preaching and our work as adult educators. Although the church often assisted the poor in their struggles for daily bread, most of the Christian leaders were reluctant, afraid or unwilling to raise a prophetic voice to lead the Haïtian people in their quest for liberation and social and economic justice. Moreover, the North American and European elitist worship styles and the message of resignation from some of the churches, particularly from the Protestant congregations, were irrelevant to the people. As lay preachers, we often expressed the need to articulate a Haïtian liberation theology but felt inadequate to undertake such a task.

Sixteen years after the passing of J. Wildès Joseph from life on earth to eternal life with Jesus Christ, the need for a Haïtian liberation theology still remains. This chapter briefly reviews the origin of liberation theology, addresses the rationale for a Haïtian liberation theology, provides a bird's eye survey of the historical context of Christianity in Haïti and proposes a two-step method for developing a Haïtian liberation theology.

> **"Although the church often assisted the poor in their struggles for daily bread, most of the Christian leaders were reluctant, afraid or unwilling to raise a prophetic voice to lead the Haïtian people in their quest for liberation and social and economic justice."**

> "Through the years, Haïti has been systematically reduced to extreme poverty by foreign powers that depleted its resources by force or threat of force and also, sadly, by its own citizens."

Rationale for a Haïtian Liberation Theology

Fwi pa tonbe lwen pyebwa
(Fruits do not fall far from the tree)

Theological reflections are never free from cultural and sociological influences. They are born in the location and the historical context of the theologians and the communities where they are developed. The Republic of Haïti, one of the two countries that share the island formerly known as Hispaniola, is considered the poorest nation in the Western Hemisphere. This land, however, has not always been poor and destitute. As P. J. Patterson, the former prime minister of Jamaica, attests, "Haïti did not jump; it was pushed over the precipice."[1] Even after Haïti's independence, won in sweat and blood, billions of dollars have been extorted from Haïti by the colonial powers that occupied its land. Haïti was once called "the pearl of the Antilles" because of its plantations, its natural resources and its industries. Through the years, Haïti has been systematically reduced to extreme poverty by foreign powers that depleted its resources by force or threat of force and also, sadly, by its own citizens.

Shortly after earning its independence from France on January 1, 1804, the United States joined France in imposing a commercial embargo on Haïti that lasted 59 years. To recognize Haïti's independence, in April 17, 1825, King Charles X of France demanded that the government of President Jean-Pierre Boyer pay to France an indemnity of 150 million gold francs in five years. This amount was later reduced to 60 million gold francs. In 2003, the payments of this indemnity, including interest, were estimated at $21 billion in current U.S. dollars.[2]

During the presidency of Nicolas Geffrard (1859–1867), Haïti provided military and financial assistance to the freedom fighters in the Dominican Republic who were seeking the independence of their country from Spain. In retaliation, the Spanish monarch threatened to send troops to Haïti unless the government paid several million dollars to Spain. In spite of strong public opinion against this action, President Geffrard conceded to avoid an invasion by Spain and a costly war.

In 1873, after a period of civil war, many foreign nationals claimed they had suffered loss and asked that the government of Nissage Saget reimburse them. Two German citizens who failed to receive the total amount they were seeking requested the intervention of their government. In response, Germany sent a war vessel to Haïti commanded by Captain Karl Batsch. Upon his arrival at the Haïtian coast, Batsch seized two small boats called *avisos* belonging to the Haïtian marines and threatened to destroy them and bomb the capital unless Haïti paid an indemnity to the German citizens and the German government. The avisos were released only after Batsch had received the amount he requested. Before leaving Haïti, the Germans pulled down the Haïtian flag and relieved themselves on it to humiliate the country and its government.

The end of the exploitation of Haïti and of its people was not yet in sight. In July of 1915, the United States used the political unrest that existed in the country as a pretext to invade Haïti. Four months later, in November, Haïti was forced to sign a treaty granting the United States complete authority over Haïti's finances, the appointment of advisers, the responsibility for es-

> **"Throughout Haïti's history of social and economic injustice, the church in Haiti was generally silent, sometimes complacent and other times an accomplice of the unjust system."**

tablishing and running public health and public works programs, supervising routine governmental affairs and creating and supervising a national gendarmerie (or police force). In 1918, the Haïtian congress approved, under threat, a constitution purportedly written by the then U.S. Assistant Secretary of the Navy, Franklin D. Roosevelt. This new constitution allowed foreigners to own land in Haïti. Such an initiative allowed American companies like Reynolds Mining to purchase land rich in natural resources, such as bauxite and copper, at a price determined by the American authorities. During the U.S. occupation, American banks became the sole lenders to the Haïtian government; loan rates were negotiated between the American authorities in Haïti and the American banks.

Unfortunately, foreign powers, such as France, Spain, Germany and the United States, were not the only culpable sources of Haïti's current demise. Haïti's own citizens have also depleted and looted its resources. Until recently, one dictator has replaced another, and military coups have been the preferred method of regime change. After their departure in 1934, U.S. troops left a national gendarmerie that remained under their control until its dissolution in 1994. This army was an instrument of repression and exploitation in the hands of the "bourgeois" upper class, composed of Mulattos and foreign nationals. As a result, the small number of rich got richer and the massive poor got poorer. Under the government of the Duvaliers, father and son, a new class of black intellectual and financial elite was born, but the situation of the poor and the oppressed did not changed.

Throughout Haïti's history of social and economic injustice, the church in Haiti was generally silent, sometimes complacent and other times an accomplice of the unjust system. Its message of resignation on earth in exchange for happiness and riches in heaven did not help the cause of the poor but did profit the oppressors.

Beginning in 1983, however, a wind of sociopolitical change and liberation began blowing in Haïti. The youth, especially university students, wanted to experience the democracy, freedom, social justice and economic equity that they had been reading about in books and watching on foreign television programs.

The church, particularly the Catholic Base Communities in the countryside and in urban ghettos, got involved in the struggle for change. This movement began on March 9, 1983, with the visit of Pope John Paul II in Haïti. Upon his arrival at the international

> **"Il faut que quelques chose change."**
> **("Something must change.")**
> —*Pope John Paul II upon arrival at the international airport in Port-au-Prince, March 9, 1983*

airport in Port-au-Prince, the Holy Father exclaimed, *"Il faut que quelques chose change"* ("Something must change."). The church heard this call and carried it to the radio waves and to street protests. This movement culminated in the departure of President-for-life Jean-Claude Duvalier to exile on February 7, 1986, in spite of the strong support of President Ronald Reagan for the Duvalier regime. Since 1983, many Haïtian theologians have talked about liberation theologies and the need for an authentic Haïtian theology, but they have not systematically articulated it.

Origin of the Theology of Liberation

The theology of liberation has its genesis in the Jewish and Christian scriptures. These sacred writings emphasize God's commitment to social justice for the poor, the orphan and the oppressed. God's plan of liberation and justice for humanity is exemplified in God's activities in human history and in the life, ministry, death and resurrection of Jesus of Nazareth. Social injustice, such as exploitation, oppression and inequitable sharing of the earth's resources, is the result of human beings' disobedience of God; it is not a part of God's plan for humanity. God's preferential option for the poor and the oppressed is expressed throughout the biblical narratives.

From the book of Genesis, one learns that God has selected some people as agents to ensure justice on earth, and God rewards them when they fulfill this mission. For instance, God chooses Abraham that "he may charge his children and his household after him to keep the way of the Lord by doing righteousness and justice; so that the Lord may bring to Abraham what [God] has promised him" (Genesis 18:19). God is always ready to hear the cry of the oppressed and to release them from bondage. When the people of Israel were being oppressed by the unjust social system of slavery in Egypt, God acted on their behalf and delivered them. "I have observed the misery of my people who are in Egypt; I have heard their cry on account of their taskmasters. Indeed, I know their sufferings, and I have come down to deliver them from the Egyptians, and to bring them up out of that land to a good and broad land" (Exodus 3:7-8).

God also empowers God's servants to raise a prophetic voice to denounce injustice and work side by side with the oppressed for a more just society. Jeremiah, Habakkuk, Amos and others cried out to the Lord and consistently reminded the people of Israel that God does not tolerate injustice. The themes of justice and liberation continue and are further developed in the New Testament. Jesus of Nazareth defined His mission in these terms: "The Spirit of the Lord is upon me, because he has anointed me to bring good news to the poor. He has sent me to proclaim release to the captive, and recovery of sight to the blind, to let the oppressed go free, and to proclaim the year of the Lord's favor" (Luke 4:18-19; also see Isaiah 61:1-2). After Jesus' death and resurrection, His disciples appropriated this mission and passed it on to Christian believers throughout the centuries. Leonardo and Clodovis Boff note:

> The roots of liberation theology are also to be found in the prophetic tradition of evangelists and missionaries from the earliest colonial days in Latin America who questioned the type of presence adopted by the church and the way indigenous peoples, blacks, mestizos, and the poor rural and urban masses were treated. The names of Bartholomé de Las Casas, Antonio de Montesinos, Antonio Vieira, Brother Caneca and others can stand for a whole host of religious personalities who have graced every century of our short history.[3]

A movement of transformation started in the churches throughout Latin America in the early 1960s. Christians, particularly Catholic brothers and sisters, started to take social mission seriously. Many young middle class men and women committed themselves to work among the poor. Charismatic priests and bishops encouraged the calls for social and political change. Various church organizations promoted understanding and improvement in the living conditions of the people. Church-based organizations, such as Young Christian Students, Young

Christian Workers, Young Christian Agriculturalists, the Movement for Basic Education and the Base Ecclesial Communities, sprang up and gave birth to a new vitality and critical spirit. The Boffs assert, "The relationship of dependence of the periphery on the center had to be replaced by a process of breaking away and liberation.

> **Liberation theology is the marriage of the Christian faith and the people's longing for social change and liberation from oppression and social injustice.**

So the basis of a theology of development was undermined and the theoretical foundations for a theology of liberation were laid."[4] Liberation theology has its origin, therefore, in a context of dialogue between the church and the Latin American societies in quest for transformation. It is the marriage of the Christian faith and the people's longing for social change and liberation from oppression and social injustice.

To articulate Latin American liberation theology, Catholic theologians such as Gustavo Gutiérrez, Segundo Galilea, Juan Luis Segundo and Leonardo Boff and Protestants such as Emilio Castro, Julio de Santa Ana and José Míguez Bonino met frequently to discuss such topics as the relationships between "faith and poverty," "gospel and social justice," and so forth. The first Catholic congress to discuss liberation theology was held in Bogotá, Colombia, in March of 1970, and the Protestants followed in 1971 in Buenos Aires, Argentina. Following these symposia, Gustavo Gutiérrez published his 1971 masterpiece *Teologia de la Liberación* (*Theology of Liberation*) and Leonardo Boff wrote a series of articles titled "Jesus Cristo Libertador" ("Jesus Christ Liberator"). These seminal works set the stage for liberation theology, a movement that Boff identifies as "a theology from the periphery dealing with the concerns of this periphery, concerns that presented and still present an immense challenge to the evangelizing of the church."[5]

A Brief History of Christianity in Haïti

As already mentioned, the history of Christianity in Haïti is closely tied to slavery, violence and injustice. Christianity arrived in Haïti with colonialism and slavery. When Christopher Columbus and the Spanish conquistadors arrived in the land they named Hispaniola on December 4, 1492, priests who came allegedly to evangelize the New World accompanied them. Columbus's first action was to plant a cross, one of the most revered symbols in the Christian faith.

> **The history of Christianity in Haïti is closely tied to slavery, violence and injustice.**

Slavery officially started in Haïti with the *encomienda* or *repartimientos* (distribution of land and indigenous people to the Spanish explorers). The *repartimientos* intensified during the government of Bobadilla, the Spanish governor sent by Queen Isabella. The *encomienderos* (receivers of grants of land and people from the Spanish Crown) had the right to exact labor or tribute from the Arawaks and, in return, were responsible for providing religious instruction to the native people and protecting them. Lewis Hanke asserts, "In theory the main objective of the laws was that the Indians [the indigenous inhabitants] might thereby be Christianized and civilized, but in fact its principal feature was that they were made to serve as slaves in the fields and

> **"The U.S. occupation of Haïti (1915–1934) considerably helped the development of Protestantism."**

mines."⁶ The hard labor imposed on the Arawaks and their exposure to European diseases exterminated almost the entire population in less than two decades.

In the French colony, religion was used as a means to pacify the African slaves. The slave masters attempted to convert the Africans to Christianity by force. In the daily life of the French colony, often there was no difference between a priest and a slave commander. The historian Jean Fouchard in the 1972 classic *Les Marrons de la Liberté* (*The Chestnuts of Freedom*) quotes a priest, Father Labbat, who caught an African practicing Vodou: "*Je fis attacher le sorcier et lui fis distribuer environ 300 coups de fouet qui l'écorchèrent depuis les épaules jusque aux genoux. Je fis mettre le sorcier aux fers après l'avoir fait laver avec une pimentade*" ("I had the sorcerer held by a post and had him flogged with 300 lashes that scorched him from his shoulders to his knees. I had him chained after being washed with a mixture of hot peppers.").⁷

After the independence of Haïti, the 1811 constitution made Catholicism the official religion of Haïti. On March 28, 1860, the Haïtian government signed a treaty with the Vatican that gave the Roman Catholic Church even more privileges in the country. After this agreement, from 1866 to the early 1950s, the Catholic Church waged a war against Vodou. Catholic priests burned Vodou shrines, beat up its priests and practitioners and destroyed their sacred vessels.

Protestantism started in Haïti as early as 1817. During the colonial period, it was forbidden for Protestants to evangelize in Haïti, but some articles of the 1811 constitution admitted the free existence of other religions in Haïti. The Methodist missionaries John Brown and James Catts arrived in Haïti in 1817. At first they wanted to evangelize the elite, but the small number of converts proved their strategy to be a mistake. They turned to the masses, who accepted Christ in great numbers. Later, the U.S. occupation of Haïti (1915–1934) considerably helped the development of Protestantism.

Developing a Haïtian Liberation Theology for Today

> *Chase sak natirèl, l'ap tounen ap galope*
> (Chase the natural, it will return galloping)

Developing a Haïtian theology of liberation cannot happen in a vacuum or on a scholar's desk. If this new breed of theology is to be Haïtian, first and foremost it must be contextual: that is, it must take the socioeconomic, political and cultural situations of the Haïtian people seriously. It must also involve theologians from Haïti or living in the Haïtian context and sharing the Haïtian experience. Furthermore, this new theological task must be the result of open and ongoing dialogue between lay- and clergypersons of all denominations and tendencies. In this context, a theologian is not necessarily seminary or Bible school trained. He or she could be anyone who reads the Bible or hears it read, reflects on it and interprets the Word of God for himself or herself, for a small group or for a community.

Doing theology requires a methodology, a process. The method one employs to articulate the gospel to Haïtians must arise from the context of the recipients' lives. In developing this theological approach, a two-step method is proposed. It includes:

> **The corruption that existed in the churches was sometimes as disgusting as that of the government.**

- A new understanding of the church, from elitism to solidarity with the people.

- A new way of doing theology that is Christ-centered and culturally relevant.

From Elitism to Solidarity With the People

The history of Haïti is marked by bravery, heroism and trailblazing endeavors. It is also characterized by violence, oppression and injustice. Too often, Haïtian church leaders have been complicit with the oppressors either by direct actions and public statements or by silence and inaction. Robert McAfee Brown notes, "The way of Columbus set the pattern, and even though some of the original excesses were later contained, the church remained hand in glove with the explorers, its leadership securely in the hands of the Spaniards."[8] The Roman Catholic Church in Haïti exemplifies that close tie with the government. The 1860 treaty between the Vatican and the Haïtian government stated, "The government of the Republic of Haïti is committed to keep and maintain an appropriate yearly allowance to the Episcopal offices from the public treasury." Although the Protestant churches had never received subvention from the government, their positions have not been more admirable. Pastors and church leaders have colluded with dictators and oppressors just as their Catholic colleagues did.

During the Duvalier regimes, some pastors and priests were also known as "*Tonton Macoutes*" (literally "bogeymen"; they served as terrifying forces of repression), others received money from the government and some were clearly among the elite who supported the oppressive regimes.

Many congregations, including Methodists, were known among the people as the church of "the bourgeoisie" (the members of the upper class). The corruption that existed in the churches was sometimes as disgusting as that of the government. Some church leaders saw themselves as the leaders of small dictatorships. They made all decisions by themselves, distributed favors to their friends and punished those whom they considered their enemies. (It is important to note that in The Methodist Church in Haïti, in particular, the current, new and emerging leaders see themselves and their role differently.)

Still today, the church leaders' collusion with the oppressors and their attitudes in society make the church look more like a political institution than a community of disciples that Jesus of Nazareth had constituted. Picture the church as a pyramid with the pastor, priest, or denominational leader at the top, a few middle managers under him (always a man), all the church's adherents at the bottom and everyone else outside. The lifestyles of the pastors are so far above that of their flock that there is a complete disconnect between the situation of the church leaders and the misery of the people. Generally, pastors in the mainline denominations do not live in the same neighborhoods as their church's members. They see themselves as an elite group that deserves to be served rather than to serve the people. Consequently, the people do not trust the church. They see its leaders as a part of the oppressive system. In this model of the church, the leaders cannot partner with Christ to lead the people toward liberation.

Developing a Haïtian liberation theology requires a new understanding of the church and its mission. Instead of *doing* church and conducting church business, priests, pastors and denominational leaders need to *be* the church, the community of believers striving to imitate Jesus Christ and serve the world, particularly "the least of these"—the poor, the orphan, the sick, the outcast and the oppressed. Leonardo and Clodovis Boff assert, "Without a minimum of suffering with, this suffering that affects the great majority of the human race, liberation theology can neither exist nor be understood.... Underlying liberation theology is a prophetic and camaraderie commitment to the life, cause, and struggle of these million of debased and marginalized human beings."[9]

> **"Instead of *doing* church, priests, pastors and denominational leaders need to *be* the church, the community of believers striving to imitate Jesus Christ and serve the world, particularly "the least of these"—the poor, the orphan, the sick, the outcast and the oppressed."**

As an institution the church will disappear, because "heaven and earth will all pass away, but my word will not pass away" (Matthew 24:35). The oppressive machines of this world can destroy buildings and kill priests, pastors and prophets as they have been doing since the first century, but they cannot eliminate the Spirit and the Word of God within believers. Archbishop Romero, a martyr for the cause of the oppressed and of Jesus Christ, captured this idea:

> If they ever take out our radio, suspended our newspapers, silence, put to death all our priests, bishops included, and you are left alone—a people without priests—then each of you will have to be a messenger, a prophet. The church will always exist as long as even one baptized person is left alive.[10]

In Archbishop Romero's view, the church is not an exclusive hierarchical organization with most of the leaders on top of a pyramid-shaped structure. To fulfill its mission "to make disciples of all nations, baptizing them in the name of the Father and of the Son and of the Holy Spirit" (Matthew 28:19) and "to bring the good news to the poor, proclaim release to the captives and recovery of sight to the blind, to let the oppressed go free" (Luke 4:18), the church needs a new understanding of itself and its mission. Rosny Desroches, a Methodist lay preacher and political activist, offered a vision of the church that can serve as a pillar to build a Haïtian liberation theology. In a sermon delivered at an ecumenical service at the Port-au-Prince Cathedral in 1985, Brother Desroches stated, "The church is the gathering of God's people in route to liberation." For that liberation to take place in Haïti, the church leaders have to abandon their elitist position and be in genuine solidarity with the people.

Solidarity and camaraderie with the people will occur only when church leaders leave the mountaintop of their privileges to come to the valley where the people are suffering from economic and social injustices. Mother Teresa of Calcutta, a Catholic nun of Albanian ethnicity and Indian citizenship, exemplified this model. Responding to her calling, Mother Teresa chose to live among the poorest of the poor in India and serve them with compassion and love. According to Kathryn Spink, Mother Teresa wrote in her diary, "Our Lord wants me to be a free nun covered with the poverty of the cross. Today I learned a good lesson.... While looking for a home, I walked and walked till my arms and legs ached. I thought how much they must ache in body and soul, looking for a home, food and health."[11] By sharing the plight of the poor, Mother Teresa was

> **"Solidarity and camaraderie with the people will occur only when church leaders leave the mountaintop of their privileges to come to the valley where the people are suffering from economic and social injustices."**

in a much better position to share the good news of salvation with them.

We see another example of Christian solidarity with the poor and the oppressed in the life and ministry of the Reverend "Sister" Paulette Holly in Haïti. The Rev. Holly, affectionately called "Sister Paulette," is a retired elder in The Methodist Church in Haïti. She was a registered nurse by profession who came from an educated and wealthy Catholic family. After her conversion to Protestantism in the Methodist Church, responding to God's call to the ministry, she abandoned a lucrative position with the government to become a deaconess in the Methodist Church. For more than four decades, Sister Paulette Holly chose to live among the poorest people in a dangerous slum in Port-au-Prince called La Saline. She served as the director of the Methodist health and dental clinic and the preacher in charge of the congregation of La Saline. In spite of her leadership roles, the people of La Saline saw Sister Paulette as one of them. The Volkswagen Beetle she drove was literally "the people's car." In addition to transporting patients from the medical clinic to the general hospital, Sister Paulette never hesitated to give a ride to anyone who asked her as long as she had room in her small car. Sister Paulette had a successful evangelistic ministry among the people of La Saline because she lived with them and shared their conditions.

The church in Haïti will have more credibility to raise a prophetic voice to cry with, and on behalf of, the masses for social justice if it lives and works in solidarity with those who are suffering. Following the example of Jesus of Nazareth and Christian disciples such as Archbishop Oscar Romero, Mother Teresa and Sister Paulette Holly will bring church leaders closer to the people they are serving. Priests, pastors and denominational leaders must utilize all the resources at their disposal to assist the people instead of building their own fortunes.

A New Way of Doing Theology

To build the foundation for a Haïtian liberation theology, Haïtian Christians must commit themselves to a new way of doing theology. After 193 years of Protestantism and 206 years of Catholicism in the Republic of Haïti since its independence, the theological approaches and the worship style in Haïti (except in some of the Catholic communities) are still modeled on European and North American patterns. It is true that these theological approaches and practices have led many Haïtians to Christ, but they are incongruent with Haïtian reality and cultural heritage. James H. Cone, the father of black theology in the African-American context, states, "Because I have lived the Bearden [Arkansas] experience, I cannot separate it from my theological perspective."[12] Similarly, the foundation of a Haïtian theology must be Christ-centered and socioculturally relevant to Haïtians.

> **"A Haïtian liberation theology must be grounded in the person of Jesus of Nazareth as the incarnation and the revelation of the one God, the creator and the redeemer of the world."**

A Christ-centered Theology

A Haïtian liberation theology must be grounded in the person of Jesus of Nazareth as the incarnation and the revelation of the one God, the creator and the redeemer of the world. In approaching Jesus the Christ, one needs to be careful to remain relevant to one's context. H. Richard Neibuhr affirmed, "Jesus Christ who is the

Haïti: Challenges and Hope | 31

Sister Paulette Holly *(umc.org/Mike Dubose)*

Christian's authority can be described, though every description falls short of completeness and must fail to satisfy others who have encountered Him."[13] This assertion is consistent with Cone's statement that "no theologian can define Jesus Christ's essence once and for all... because all theological statements are limited by the theologian's cultural standpoint."[14]

As the divine presence, the Emmanuel, "God with us," Jesus is not subject to human beings' theological concepts and limitations. The centrality of Jesus Christ in a theology developed by Haïtians for Haïtians would be nothing less than liberating, because Jesus of Nazareth is the liberator of the world. Jesus' life, ministry and death resonate with the life circumstances of the Haïtian people who are victims of oppression and injustice. His resurrection from the dead is a reality that gives hope for their liberation and salvation.

Jesus' ministry took place in the shadow of military occupation, violence, social unrest and oppression of the poor. In that context Jesus used the oracle of the prophet Isaiah to define His mission: "The Spirit of the Lord is upon me, because he has anointed me to bring good news to the poor. He has sent me to proclaim release to the captives and recovery of sight to the blind, to let the oppressed go free, to proclaim the year of the Lord's favor" (Luke 4:18-19). Gene L. Davenport reflects on the gospel of Jesus Christ: "The gospel is the proclamation of the presence of freedom, the reality of love, the movement of peace and the establishment of justice. These are not to be contemplated, debated or respected, but

> **"Jesus' ministry took place in the shadow of military occupation, violence, social unrest and oppression of the poor."**

accepted, appropriated, lived and manifested."[15] A Haïtian theology grounded in a Christology that is consistent with that vision is therefore a liberating theology.

The ministry of Sister Paulette Holly in Haïti was Christ-centered because not only was Jesus the Christ the central figure of her teaching and preaching but also because she exemplified in her daily activities, the life of simplicity, service and self-sacrifice that Jesus gave us. Sister Paulette could have lived a comfortable life away from the suffering and misery of the poor and come on Sundays to preach from the elevated pulpit as some of her colleagues in the country did. Instead, she chose to proclaim Christ not only in words but also in deeds, by living and working in La Saline with the poor and destitute. Sister Paulette was not theologizing but was living a Christ-centered theology.

A Culturally Relevant Theology

H. Richard Neibuhr broadly defined culture as the process and total result of human beings' endeavors that comprise "language, habit, idea, belief, custom, social organization, inherited artifacts, technical process, and values."[16] The Haïtian culture is a symbiosis of West African, French, Spanish and American cultures. There were, and are, significant differences between

> **"Conversion meant not only renouncing sin and the forces of evil, coming to Jesus Christ and beginning a lifelong journey of discipleship; it also meant renouncing one's cultural identity."**

the urban and rural areas. The rural areas are more traditional and thus bear more resemblance to West African villages, whereas urban areas are more inclined toward European and North American cultures. Until the 1980s, Haïtian culture was influenced about 70 percent by African cultures, 20 percent French and 10 percent American and Spanish cultures. Currently, there is a cultural shift toward the hip-hop culture of the United States, particularly among the youth, but the African cultural heritage is still dominant.

The theologies that the European and the North American missionaries brought to Haïti typify what Richard Neibuhr called "Christ-against-culture." The missionaries and their Haïtian successors equated nearly everything that came from Africa with Vodou and saw it as evil. Traditional African musical instruments, such as drums, bamboo and *tchatcha,* were replaced with organs and pianos. The upbeat rhythms of the people were replaced with classical tunes. Conversion meant not only renouncing sin and the forces of evil, coming to Jesus Christ and beginning a lifelong journey of discipleship; it also meant renouncing one's cultural identity. Being a true Christian required living like the missionaries, wearing a suit or a jacket in church and uncovering one's head (for men). Under the cover of proclaiming a gospel free from the Haïtian cultural influence (or Vodou influence), the missionaries actually were proclaiming a gospel permeated by their own cultural biases. It is still not uncommon to see a Haïtian man wearing a suit and tie to preach outdoors or in a metal-roofed building without air-conditioning in 98 degree Fahrenheit heat.

The gospel of Jesus Christ is "above culture" in the sense that it transcends the limitations of history to reach men, women and children where they are in their sociocultural contexts. At the same time, it is received and practiced in the believer's location and context. A Haïtian liberation theology must take both—the universality of Jesus Christ as the revelation of God in human history and the sociocultural realities of the Haïtian people—seriously. This way of doing theology must employ the Haïtian culture as a vehicle to communicate the good news of liberation and salvation in Jesus Christ to Haïtians. The high rate of illiteracy in Haïti suggests that songs, symbols and dramatization are the best means for transmitting theological beliefs and doctrinal concepts. In addition, a Haïtian liberation theology must make use of African dances, such as the Yanvalou, the Congo, the Maïs, the Petro, the Ibo *and* the Nago, in worship services to communicate the message of love, compassion and mercy of the gospel. Hymns and songs using imagery of the oppressor's cultural reality, such as "*blanc, plus blanc que neige*" (white, whiter than snow), must be replaced with images familiar to Haïtian worshipers and taken from their environment. Storytelling in the African and Haïtian traditions must become a part of the teaching and preaching of the gospel. Musical instruments, such as the Bamboo, *tchatcha* and the African drum, must be given their due place in worship services and other Christian gatherings for the glory of the triune God and for the spiritual and emotional renewal of Haïtian communities. The evangelistic task of the church in Haïti demands that the presentation of the gospel be culturally relevant to Haïtians.

Conclusion

Theological reflections are never culture-free or neutral. As human beings' reflections, understanding and interpretation about God, theology is born out of the sociocultural and historical contexts of the theologians and of the community where it is developed. The ancient Hebrews enslaved in Egypt or in captivity in Babylon saw God as the liberator who would set them

> **"The evangelistic task of the church in Haïti demands that the presentation of the gospel be culturally relevant to Haïtians."**

free from oppression and take them to the Promised Land. They expected the coming of God's Messiah who would lead them to freedom and liberation. The early Christians hoped for the imminent return of the *Parousia*, the second coming of Jesus Christ as King of Kings and Lord of Lords to deliver them from persecution and oppression and take them with Him into the kingdom of God. For the church to remain a credible instrument of God's justice and a witness for Jesus Christ, it has to be relevant to the life of the people it exists to serve. If the church in Haïti—Protestant and Roman Catholic, connectional as well as independent—wants to be relevant to the Haïtian people, it has to address their needs and concerns. It must accompany them in their quest for social and economic justice. The priests, pastors and church leaders must be in solidarity with the people—live with them, suffer with them and experience their lives—in order to participate in and lead them in their struggle for social and economic justice.

Complacency and the complicity of many Christian leaders with the oppressive system, the internal corruption and the division among the leaders of the church all work to make their position, at best, suspicious to the people. Too many stories are true of church leaders and managers of church-based organizations gaining personal wealth from the assistance they are receiving on behalf of the needy. The Christian faith is not so much about orthodoxy, or right beliefs, but about orthopraxy, or right actions. Protestant pastors and Roman Catholic priests cannot ask their parishioners to do what they say and then not follow their own example. As part of the dialogue to develop a Haïtian liberation theology, the church has to repent of its sins and clean up its institutions in order to be trusted by the people and be relevant to their lives.

The theological reflections that will lead toward a Haïtian liberation theology must take place in a context of dialogue among lay and clergy theologians of all tendencies and denominations interested in accompanying the people in their struggle for a better life. A Haïtian liberation theology articulated by Haïtians and other theologians living in Haïtian contexts will not take place overnight. It will be the result of a process of development, adjustment and readjustment where every thinker will add his or her contribution.

Jules Casséus provides a fine contextual reflection on the sociopolitical and ecclesiastical events in Haïti from February 1986 to February 1991. His book *Haïti: Quelle Èglise . . . Quelle Liberation?* (*Haïti: What Church . . . What Liberation?*) introduces the need for a Haïtian theology and encourages church leaders to pay heed to the people's cry. It is my hope and prayer that more Haïtian theologians and others sharing the Haïtian experience will make further contributions to the development of a Haïtian liberation theology until it is fully articulated and lived.

Notes

1. P. J. Patterson's March 15, 2010, speech to the St Lucia's Civil Response Committee to the emergency in Haïti as the special representative of CARICOM to Haïti.
2. "France's Debt to Haïti," *Haïti Progrès* 12, no. 31 (October 15–21, 2003).
3. Clodovis Boff and Leonardo Boff, *Introducing Liberation Theology* (Maryknoll, N.Y.: Orbis Books, 1987), 66.
4. Ibid., 68.
5. Ibid.

6. Lewis Hanke, *The Spanish Struggle for Justice in the Conquest of America* (Boston: Little Brown & Company, 1966), 20.
7. Jean Fouchard, *Les Marrons de la Liberté* (Paris: Edition de l'École, 1972), 112.
8. Robert McAfee Brown, *Liberation Theology: An Introductory Guide* (Louisville, Ky.: Westminster/John Knox, 1993), 70.
9. Boff and Boff, *Introducing Liberation Theology*, 3.
10. As quoted in Brown, *Liberation Theology*, 69.
11. Kathryn Spink, *Mother Teresa: A Complete Authorized Biography* (San Francisco: HarperSanFrancisco, 1987), 37.
12. James H. Cone, *God of the Oppressed* (Maryknoll, N.Y.: Orbis Books, 1997), 4.
13. H. Richard Neibuhr, *Christ and Culture* (New York: HarperCollins Publishers, 1996), 14.
14. Cone, *God of the Oppressed*, 81.
15. G. L. Davenport, *Into the Darkness* (Nashville: Abingdon Press, 1988), 38.
16. Neibuhr, *Christ and Culture*, citing Bronislaw Malinowski, "Culture" in *Encyclopedia of Social Sciences* (vol. IV), 621 ff.

A woman carries a bundle past a collapsed building in Port-au-Prince, Haïti *(Paul Jeffrey)*

Chapter Three
Gone in 35 Seconds:
The 35 Seconds That Changed Haïti's Landscape

> *Lanmò pa gen klaksòn*
> (Death does not have a warning bell)
>
> *L'anmò pa respekte pèsonn*
> (Death respects no one)

September 11, 2001, is a date that will remain in the American psyche for a very long time. Most U.S. citizens remember where they were and what they were doing when they received the news of the terrorist attack in New York City. The scope of the destruction and the unprecedented number of casualties (nearly 3,000 deaths) made this tragedy memorable. Could you imagine a disaster about 800 times greater than the September 11 attack? This is exactly what happened in Haïti on January 12, 2010.

Comparing the terrorist attack in the United States and the earthquake in Haïti might be seen by some readers as "comparing apples to oranges" because the former was a human-made catastrophe and the latter a natural disaster. They are, however, used in comparison to introduce this chapter because of the similar emotional impact they had, and continue to have, on people in the United States and Haïti. Just as the people of the United States understand what 9/11 means in their lives, Haïtians know and will always remember what 1/12/10 means.

January 12, 2010, began as a normal busy Tuesday. Students, wearing their clean, colorful and beautiful uniforms, went to school cheerful and giggling. Young men and women, alone or in the company of friends and peers, full of dreams for a better tomorrow, drove, walked and rode to the overcrowded universities and technical schools. Professionals, artisans and laborers all went to work to provide for their families as they normally did, unsuspecting what the day would bring them. None of them knew that their lives would be drastically changed forever.

In the afternoon, many had just reached home from a busy day; others were looking at the clock, waiting for a few more minutes to sign out; others were still in the middle of learning, teaching, making presentations, cutting, sewing, cooking, ironing and accomplishing thousands of other routine tasks. Suddenly, at 4:53 p.m., something incredulous began happening. Books on shelves and decorations on walls were falling down, pieces of furniture were moving and doors were opening and closing by themselves. People on the streets and

Haïti: Challenges and Hope | 37

A soldier from the U.S. Second Airborne Division surveys damage inside the Cathedral of Our Lady of the Assumption in Port-au-Prince, Haïti. *(Paul Jeffrey)*

in automobiles watched buildings collapse like castles made of cards. A powerful 7.0 magnitude earthquake hit the Département de L'Ouest (the Western Department) that includes Port-au-Prince, Delmas, Petion-Ville, Carrefour, Léogâne, Grand-Goâve, Petit-Goâve and many other surrounding cities.

It took only 35 seconds for humble houses, impressive and luxurious buildings, national monuments, fancy hotels and majestic cathedrals to be reduced to piles of rubble. Beloved homes and buildings that offered protection and safety a few seconds earlier were transformed into killing machines and tombs. It happened so fast that thousands of people perished without even knowing what hit them.

The Scope of the Devastation

Haïti is situated in the middle of the Caribbean Sea and the Atlantic Ocean. This strategic location places the country in the path of many violent storms and hurricanes. Through the years, Haïti has had more than its share of catastrophes. As a result of years of deforestation, the absence of adequate building codes or lack of enforcement by the authorities and the nonexistence of comprehensive urban planning, Haïti has experienced numerous deadly floods, mudslides and storms.

In 2004, tropical storm Jeanne killed an estimated 3,000 people when swollen rivers of rock and mud rushed down exposed mountains. Most of the victims were in the city of Gonaïves, located 148 kilometers from Port-au-Prince. In 2008, about 800 people died and nearly 60 percent of the country's harvest was destroyed when four powerful storms struck Haïti within 30 days. Nevertheless, none of these disasters could have prepared the country for the scope of the January 12 earthquake.

Five months after the quake, when this book was being written, there were still no viable statistics about the number of people killed. There are many reasons to explain this lack of information. One of them is that the authorities were completely stunned by the scope of

Port-au-Prince after the earthquake. *(Paul Jeffrey)*

the destruction. A few days after the earthquake, bodies were carried by truckloads and dumped into mass graves without being identified. There were no pictures, fingerprints or DNA samples taken for later identification and statistical records. After waiting for days for bodies to be picked up by the authorities, people took matters into their own hands and burned decomposed bodies near their homes. As of July 2010, thousands of bodies were still buried under rubble.

In 35 seconds, Haïti's landscape, particularly the areas that were directly hit by the earthquake, changed forever. Millions of lives have been affected. It is estimated that over 300,000 people were killed and a similar number injured. The earthquake also left about 4,000 amputees who will carry the scars forever. Thousands of children became orphans. In addition to the loss of life and the wounds sustained, people have also lost their life savings, their inheritances, the houses they grew up in or raised their children in. More than 250,000 homes were destroyed and many more were damaged. Careers, wages and dreams were left in the dust of the collapsed buildings.

An estimated 400,000 people have left the metropolitan area and relocated to other departments and cities, such as Jérémie, Port-de-Paix and Cap Haïtian, that were not affected by the earthquake. Over 1,000,000 people became homeless, and many more were traumatized.

The People's Solidarity

The January 12, 2010, earthquake brought an outpouring of much needed international attention to Haïti. Governments, institutions and individuals from all over the world came to help the people of Haïti deal with the greatest catastrophe they have ever faced. Many have raised funds or have made personal monetary or in-kind contributions for the victims. However, before the international television channels were able to broadcast images of the destruction, before the cries for help were

Haïti: Challenges and Hope | 39

A family in the Haïtian village of Dabonne stands in front of the temporary shelter they built following the destruction of their home in the January 12 earthquake. They used old lumber salvaged from the ruins of their previous house. *(Paul Jeffrey)*

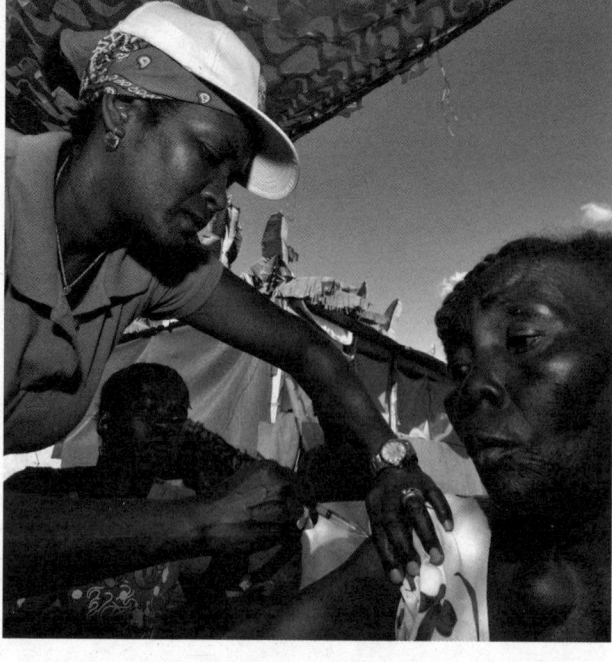

A survivor of the January 12 earthquake in Leogane, Haïti (right), still suffers from a broken collarbone and receives an injection from Marisol Baez, a nurse from the Dominican Republic who works as a promoter for the Dominican-Haïtian Women's Movement (MUDHA). *(Paul Jeffrey)*

A woman digs with a machete as she builds a temporary home in a spontaneous camp for quake survivors being established in Croix-des-Bouquets, Haïti, north of the capital Port-au-Prince. *(Paul Jeffrey)*

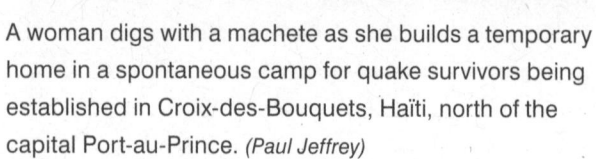

A survivor of the January 12 earthquake gives her daughter a bath amidst the rubble in the Port-au-Prince neighborhood of Belair. Water remains in short supply following the devastating quake. *(Paul Jeffrey)*

Women line up for food from the World Food Program during a massive distribution in Port-au-Prince, Haïti. *(Paul Jeffrey)*

(top) A woman fastens sticks together with strips of cloth as she builds a temporary home in a spontaneous camp for quake survivors being established in Croix-des-Bouguets, Haïti, north of the capital Port-au-Prince. *(Paul Jeffrey)*

(right) Silvani Joseph, 48, survived the January 12, 2010, earthquake and carries debris as she and her neighbors begin to build temporary shelters in the Port-au-Prince neighborhood of Belair. *(Paul Jeffrey)*

Haïti: Challenges and Hope | 41

A "tent city" of homeless earthquake survivors in the Bobin neighborhood of Port-au-Prince, Haïti. *(Paul Jeffrey)*

Participants in a Port-au-Prince worship service for survivors of the January 12 earthquake that ravaged the Caribbean nation. *(Paul Jeffrey)*

heard on YouTube and on social networks, the Haïtian people displayed extraordinary signs of solidarity with their neighbors and countrypersons.

Minutes after the earthquake struck, many people were so shocked by the scope of the destruction that they could do nothing other than fall on their knees to confess their sins and thank God for being alive. Others were baffled and wondered why this disaster happened and why they were alive. After the initial shock, however, the people of Haïti quickly displayed an extraordinary spirit of solidarity and selflessness toward victims trapped in collapsed buildings. Men, women and sometimes even children, armed with their bare hands, machetes, hammers, shovels and occasionally handsaws, started to attack the murderous concrete and iron bars that once helped to secure their buildings. They desperately and steadfastly worked to save a mother, a child, a parent, a friend, a neighbor, a coworker, or a total stranger.

Without spending hours in meetings to go over risk analyses, without thinking about their own lives or well-being, they worked tirelessly day and night to rescue many who would have died without their help. The rationale that many of these heroes gave for risking their lives was, "We were there and someone needed our help." The devastation has shed light on many unnamed heroes. It is interesting that, in spite of the numerous selfless actions and heroic rescues, none has described himself or herself as a hero.

The tremendous courage, resiliency and solidarity shown by the Haïtian people after this dreadful day make one proud to be a Haïtian or to have a Haïtian parent or grandparent. It gives one hope that, once again, with genuine compassion and assistance from people around the world, Haïti shall overcome this disaster with God's grace.

Men in earthquake-ravaged Port-au-Prince dig into the rubble of a building, hoping to find the remains of 20 people they believe are buried inside. *(Paul Jeffrey)*

In Port-au-Prince, Don Tatlock, an emergency worker for Church World Service, a member of the ACT Alliance, unloads tons of relief material brought into earthquake-ravaged Haïti from the Dominican Republic on January 25, 2010.
(Paul Jeffrey)

Chapter Four
Links of Solidarity and Partnership

> *Men anpil chay pa lou*
> (Many hands make weight light)

Haïtians and friends of Haïti are grateful for the outpouring of support the country has received following the devastating 7.0 magnitude earthquake on January 12, 2010. Many nations, institutions and individuals around the world have been touched by the unfortunate plight of Haïti and mobilized in an unprecedented way to express solidarity with the Haïtian people. From politicians and superstars to ordinary citizens and schoolchildren, from wealthy foundations to small churches, people made donations and raised funds to provide immediate assistance to the survivors and help in the long rebuilding process.

In addition to the European Union and countries such as the United States, Canada and France, who gave or promised considerable amounts to aid the earthquake survivors, by the end of March 2010, about 24 countries in Africa had either donated or pledged millions of dollars for Haïtian relief efforts. Of course the amount represents a tiny fraction of the total of $5.3 billion promised worldwide to be delivered within 18 months. Nonetheless, for the continent with the world's highest poverty rates, this generosity was notable and well appreciated. Among the largest contributions from African governments was a pledge of $3 million from Ghana, $5 million from Nigeria, $2 million from Equatorial Guinea and a donation of $2.5 million from the Democratic Republic of Congo (DRC).[1] The CARICOM (Caribbean Community) nations and many Latin American countries have also enthusiastically responded and expressed solidarity with the Haïtian people. From Venezuela to Brazil, from Chile to Costa Rica, from Ecuador to the neighboring Dominican Republic, from Bolivia to Mexico, from Jamaica to Saint Lucia, all have shown support for Haïti in one way or another.

It is important to mention that the people of Cuba and their government provided tremendous assistance to Haïti and had been doing so long before the January 12 tragedy. Since 1998, the Cuban government has sent doctors, paramedics and health technicians to work in Haïti. An estimated 6,000 Cuban health care professionals have served as volunteers throughout Haïti for extended periods of time. In addition, 450 young Haïtians have graduated from Cuban medical schools free of charge. At the time of the earthquake, over 400 Cuban specialists, including 344 medical doctors and paramedics, were working in Haïti in a joint venture between the United Nations and the Cuban government.

In the first hours after the quake, before any other international team could travel to Haïti, including the Venezuelans who arrived on the ground in Haïti the next day, the Cuban medical teams and the Haïtians were the first responders rescuing and providing care to victims.

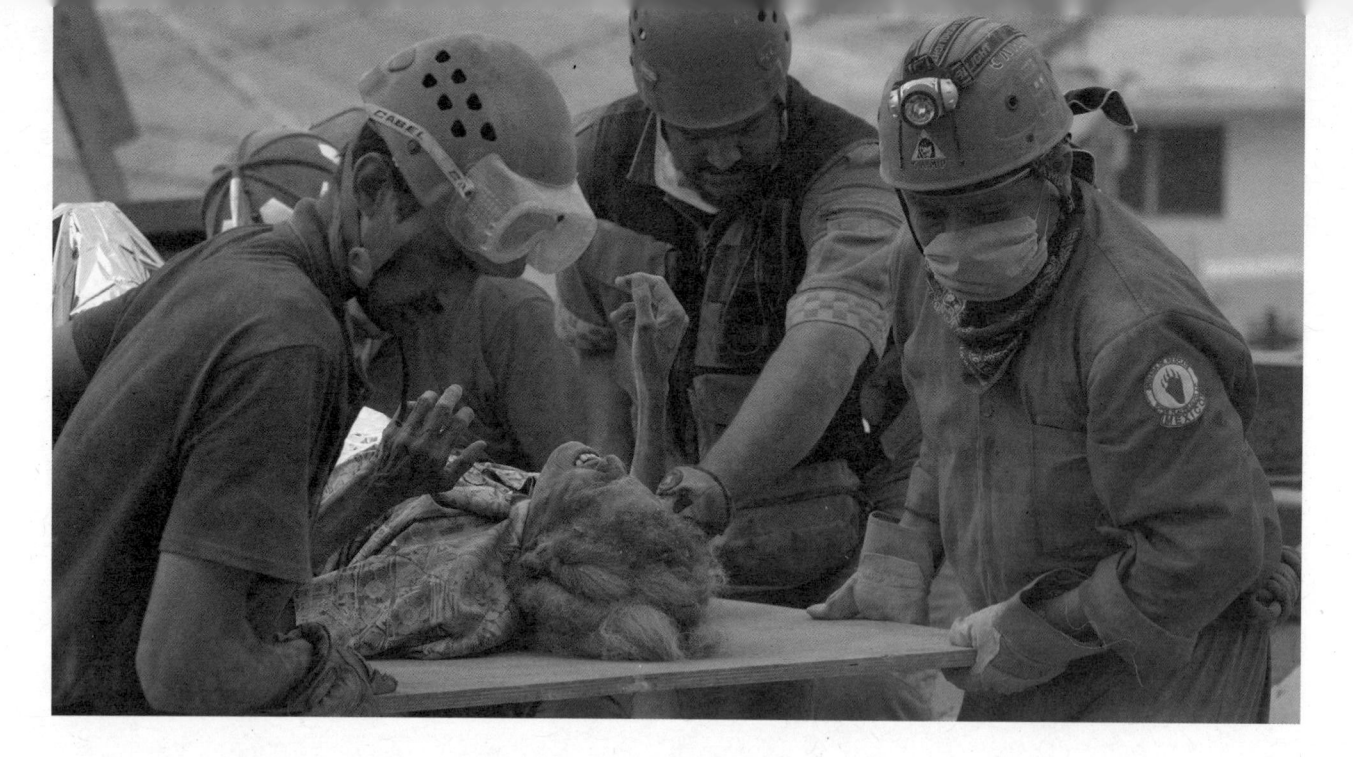

Anna Zizi is pulled alive on January 19 from the rubble of Haïti's devastating earthquake, one week after the city was reduced to ruins in a matter of seconds. She was rescued from the collapsed home of the parish priest at Port-au-Prince's Roman Cathedral of Our Lady of the Assumption by members of a Mexican search and rescue team, several of whom were in tears as they pulled the woman free from tons of rubble. *(Paul Jeffrey)*

In addition to the medical personnel who were already in Haïti, the Cuban leader Raul Castro dispatched another team of 60 medical doctors and health technicians to assist in caring for the victims. In spite of their limited resources, the Cuban authorities donated many tons of medications to treat the injured. They acted magnanimously, putting aside international political rivalry and allowed the United States Army to use their restricted air space for the medical evacuations of earthquake victims.

As of August 2010, over seven months since the earthquake, donor countries were slow in the disbursement of aid pledges. Former U.S. President Bill Clinton, the United Nations special envoy to Haïti, noted, "International donors are still reluctant to make good on billions of dollars in pledges for Haïti's post-earthquake reconstruction."[2] According to the Associated Press, $506 million had been disbursed, less than 10 percent of pledges, and only 29 percent of this has gone to the government of Haïti. This amount has been given by only five countries: Brazil, Norway, Australia, Colombia and Estonia. On July 29, U.S. President Barack Obama signed a law approving $770 million for Haïti reconstruction, but at the end of August, lawmakers were still debating how the money would be spent. Meanwhile, over a million Haïtians are still living under fraying tents and tarps as the hurricane season picks up. (See Appendix A for an article on emergency shelters.)

Ongoing Relationship Between The United Methodist Church and The Methodist Church in Haïti

> *Se nan malè ou konnen ki moun ki zanmi w*
> (It is in adversity you recognize your true friends)

The United Methodist Church has a long-standing relationship with the people of Haïti through The Methodist Church in Haïti and other institutions working in the country. This relationship has been carried out through agencies, such as the United Methodist Committee on Relief (UMCOR), the United Methodist Volunteers-in-Mission (UMVIM) and other General Board of

> **"In the months following the earthquake, dozens of UMVIM teams were in standby to go into Haïti."**

Global Ministries programs, including United Methodist Women and annual conferences, such as West Michigan, Detroit and Florida. In addition, individual and local congregations from many annual conferences have maintained partnerships with individual congregations, schools and clinics for many years.

In 2005, the UMCOR NGO established a permanent office in Haïti with the aim of assisting the victims of the devastating hurricane Jeanne that killed more than 3,000 people and caused significant damage to crops and other properties. The Haïti office sponsored sustainable economic activities aimed at improving the living conditions of the population. In the region of Dondon, near Cap Haïtian in the Northern Department, for instance, UMCOR funding to the Dondon Agriculture Development Assistance Project helps farmers improve their productivity by providing them with seeds and tools as well as technical assistance. This project was also instrumental in reintroducing Creole pigs to the community. UMCOR has also supported the Hot Lunch program that provides meals to the children enrolled in Methodist schools throughout the country. It also distributed hundreds of school kits to schoolchildren and continues to do so.

In response to the January 12 earthquake, UMCOR has intensified its cooperation with The Methodist Church in Haïti. The Haïti UMCOR NGO office that closed in 2008 has been reopened in collaboration with Haïtian church leaders to provide assistance to the victims. At the time this study was being written, a church liaison was being hired to work more closely with the leaders of The Methodist Church in Haïti and assist in the coordination of work-team volunteers and local church projects in Haïti. UMCOR was also meeting with representatives from The Methodist Church in Haïti, the United Church of Canada and the Methodist Church of Britain to envision new postearthquake development programs that will include services related to agriculture, micro-credit and micro-enterprise, health, literacy and adult education.

For many years, United Methodist Volunteers-in-Mission has been coordinating work teams from local United Methodist congregations throughout the United States traveling to Haïti to work in construction projects and medical clinics as well as in other areas of need identified by The Methodist Church in Haïti. In the months following the earthquake, dozens of UMVIM teams were in standby to go into Haïti. In June of 2010, UMCOR and UMVIM Jurisdictional Coordinators were still assessing the damage and prioritizing future projects. They proposed a three-year plan to facilitate the work of volunteer teams for projects identified as a priority by The Methodist Church in Haïti. (See Appendix B, "Haïti Response Project Overview," or visit UMVIM's website, http://new.gbgm-umc.org/about/us/mv/Haiti/plan/.)

United Methodist Women is known throughout the United Methodist connection for its missionary and social justice ministries in the world. For many years prior to the earthquake, United Methodist Women was working with The Methodist Church in Haïti and other organizations in the country. In addition to their work with the Methodist women in Haïti to strengthen their ministry and involvement in the church, United Methodist Women has supported many projects led by The Methodist Church in Haïti and by other nonprofit organizations, including funding for Grace Children's Hospital, one of the health care facilities in Port-au-Prince. It also provides financial support to groups such as Haïtian Artisans for Peace International (HAPI). This organization is the first Latin American "Communities of Shalom" (COS) initiative in partnership with Drew University COS and as a sister COS to the Grand Rapids District COS. (See Appendix C for information about HAPI's programs and the Communities of Shalom.)

The ongoing relationship between The United Methodist Church and The Methodist Church in Haïti is also exemplified in the partnership agreements signed between United Methodist annual conferences and The Methodist Church in Haïti. The Detroit and West Michigan Annual Conferences (see Appendix D) and the Florida Annual Conference (see Appendix E) are among the agencies that have signed agreements with The Methodist Church in Haïti.

The Haïti–Michigan Covenant

The West Michigan and Detroit Conferences have been working with individual churches, schools and local projects in The Methodist Church in Haïti for many years. This relationship was formalized in 1996 with the signing of a Covenant Partnership between these annual conferences and The Methodist Church in Haïti, a District Conference of the Methodist Church in the Americas and the Caribbean (MCCA). This covenant states, "Cooperative projects and programs in which the Michigan Area conferences enter will be those initiated by the Haïti District, Église Méthodiste d'Haïti of the Methodist Churches in the Caribbean and Americas and in accord with the General Board of Global Ministries and the United Methodist Committee on Relief (UMCOR)."

> **United Methodist Women is known throughout the United Methodist connection for its missionary and social justice ministries in the world.**

For more than 14 years, the Michigan Area annual conferences have been working on various projects to assist The Methodist Church in Haïti in its outreach ministries to serve and witness to the people of Haïti. The Michigan Area Haïti Task Force (MAHTF)[3] has endeavored to support, among others, the following ministry initiatives in Haïti:

- The Methodist Schools Hot Lunch Program.

- The "Water Ministry" of the Bio-Sand Water Filter Program.

- The orientation and coordination of Volunteers-in-Mission teams going to Haïti from the Michigan Area.

- Collaboration with other United Methodist conferences to fulfill projects requested and initiated by The Methodist Church in Haïti.

Since the devastating earthquake, the Michigan Area conferences have intensified their collaboration and ministries with The Methodist Church in Haïti with the aim of bringing much needed support to the people of Haïti. They have raised about $500,000 to support the earthquake victims; they continue to be the primary contributors to the Methodist Schools Hot Lunch Program. (See the full text of the covenant agreement at Appendix D.)

The Haïti–Florida Covenant

More than two million Haïtians live in the diaspora (scattered around the world) and more than 850,000 of them call the United States home. The State of Florida has one of the largest concentrations of Haïtians in the United States. An estimated 300,000 people of Haïtian origin live in Florida, and most of them reside in South Florida. It should not be surprising, therefore, that among the 63 annual conferences of The United Methodist Church in the United States, the Florida Annual Conference has a unique relationship with Haïtians and Haïti.

The Florida Annual Conference has been in ministry directly with the Haïtian population since the early 1980s. Its commitment to the newly arrived Haïtians to Florida started to take shape when Luc Dessieux,[4] a primary school teacher and a lay member of The Methodist Church in Haïti moved to South Florida and joined Grace United Methodist Church, located in the area that became known as Little Haïti in Miami. Shortly after joining Grace UMC, in 1981, Dessieux sought and received approval to start a Creole worship service in the church's fellowship hall to service the spiritual needs of his fellow refugees. This marked the beginning of the Haïtian ministries in the Florida Annual Conference. From these humble beginnings, the Florida Conference Haïtian Ministries has grown tremendously and now includes more than 19 congregations and houses of worship. (See Appendix F for an article on the Institute of Preaching.) Today, in addition to Florida, United Methodists of Haïtian origin are worshiping in Haïtian congregations located in Georgia, New Jersey, New York, Maryland, Massachusetts, California and other states.

The Florida Annual Conference ministries with Haïtians residing in Florida have been expanding to reach out to those living in Haïti and worshiping in

The Rev. Dr. Jacques Pierre (center, standing) gives the morning devotions at the Institute of Preaching in Port-au-Prince. *(The Rev. Linda Standifer)*

Haïti: Challenges and Hope | 49

congregations of The Methodist Church in Haïti. A close partnership has developed between The Methodist Church in Haïti and the Florida Annual Conference under the leadership of Bishop Timothy Whitaker; the Rev. Raphael Dessieu, then president of The Methodist Church in Haïti; and other lay- and clergypersons serving the Florida Annual Conference and in The Methodist Church in Haïti. This bilateral relationship was consolidated in June 2006 by the signing of a covenant between The Methodist Church in Haïti and The Florida Annual Conference of The United Methodist Church. Although the two church communities were already sharing in ministry, the signing of the covenant enabled them to work together more efficiently. It also created structures that facilitate communication and promote understanding and mutual respect, which lead to better coordination and exchanges in ministries.

Through the ministries of the United Methodist Committee on Relief and the United Methodist Volunteers-in-Mission, the entire United Methodist connection, particularly the churches in the United States, have been providing support to the people of Haïti since the January 12, 2010, earthquake that destroyed most of Port-au-Prince and many neighboring cities in the western region. In addition to other contributions made to UMCOR for the earthquake victims, during the 2010 annual conference session, the Florida Annual Conference collected about $130,000 for The Methodist Church in Haïti to assist in the immediate relief and with pastors' salaries. At the end of May 2010, during a visit to Haïti, some leaders of the Florida Annual Conference saw for themselves the scope of the earthquake devastation. As a result, they explored ways to provide long-term assistance to the Methodist Church and other non-church-related organizations in Haïti. (See the full text of the covenant agreement at Appendix E.)

Avenues for Partnership With Haïti

> *L'Union fait la force*
> (Unity makes strength)
>
> *Yon sèl nou fèb, ansanm nou fò*
> (Alone we are weak,
> but together we are strong)

After reading or hearing about so much need in Haïti, the reader may feel powerless and wonder, "What can someone like me do to help?" Or you might feel defeated and overwhelmed, "One person cannot change anything in this horrible situation." If these are the thoughts going through your mind, consider the motto printed on the Haïtian insignia, *"L'Union Fait la Force"* ("Unity Makes Strength") or this Creole saying, *"Yon sèl nou fèb, ansanm nou fò"* ("Alone we are weak, but together we are strong.").

It is understandable to feel overwhelmed by so much destruction, human suffering and need, but none of us is powerless. By joining with other children of God, each one of us, regardless of our age or financial means, can make a difference and give hope to our sisters and brothers in Haïti. In addition to praying for the people of Haïti and The Methodist Church in Haïti, here are some of the avenues through which individuals and groups can respond to God's call, "Whom shall I send? Who will go for us?"

- Support United Methodist Women Mission Giving opportunities as we continue to work with women, children and youth in Haïti. For more information visit www.unitedmethodistwomen.org.

- Make a donation to the United Methodist Committee on Relief (UMCOR) Advance Special Haïti Emergency #4118325. Make donations online at www.umcorHaïti.org; through regular local church or annual conference offerings when the fund is designated to Haïti Advance #4118325; by check made payable to UMCOR and addressed to P.O. Box 9068, New York, NY 10087; or by credit card at 1-800-554-8583.

- Contact the disaster response coordinator at your local church or your annual conference to learn how to organize a mission team to go to Haïti.

- Volunteer to be a part of a mission team going to Haïti.

- Prepare health/hygiene kits to be sent to Haïti and encourage others in your United Methodist Women units or local churches to do the same. Each kit should contain the following items:

  » 1 hand towel (15" x 25" up to 17" x 27", no kitchen towels)
  » 1 washcloth
  » 1 comb (large and sturdy, not pocket-sized)
  » 1 nail file or fingernail clippers (no emery boards or toenail clippers)
  » 1 bath-size bar of soap (3 oz. and up)
  » 1 toothbrush (single brushes only in original wrapper, no child-size brushes)
  » 6 adhesive plastic strip sterile bandages
  » $1.00 to purchase toothpaste

- A United Methodist Women unit or a local church may adopt a sister church in The Methodist Church in Haïti. Talk with your pastor first, then contact your district or your annual conference for information on how to proceed.

Notes

1. See March 31, 2010, articles on the International Donors' Conference for Haïti, including "African Countries Pledge Assistance to Haïti" (The United Nations Development Programme site, http://content.undp.org/go/newsroom. Figures from DRC and Nigeria from "African Countries Pledge Assistance to Haïti." Also see http://wapedia.mobi/en/Humanitarian_response_by_national_governments_to_the_2010_Haiti_earthquake#11.
2. Jonathan M. Katz, "Clinton: Donors Still Holding Out on Haïti Pledges," The Associated Press, August 6, 2010.
3. See the website of the Michigan Area Haïti Task Force at http://www.stovern.net/Haiti/ for more information.
4. The Reverend Luc Dessieux is now an ordained elder serving a Haïtian-American congregation in the Florida Annual Conference of The United Methodist Church.

A woman left homeless by Haïti's January 12 earthquake lives in a makeshift tent city in the yard of a partially destroyed school in Port-au-Prince. The quake left hundreds of thousands of people homeless. The ACT Alliance has installed a water system in the camp where she lives. *(Paul Jeffrey)*

Chapter Five
Challenges and Opportunities for Haïti and Its People

Apre lapli gen bon tan
(After the rain comes the sunshine)

The 7.0 magnitude earthquake that hit Haïti's capital and most of its western area brought unprecedented destruction, human tragedy and humanitarian crisis to the country. Unfortunately, however, Haïti's precarious situation and the majority of its people's suffering predate the January 12, 2010, earthquake. This chapter presents an overview of the challenges Haïti was facing prior to the devastating earthquake and highlights the new challenges brought by this most recent catastrophe. It also points to the new opportunities created by this tragedy.

Haïti's Challenges Prior to the January 12 Earthquake

Systematic plunder of the country's resources by the European and North American powers that colonized and occupied Haïti throughout its history and by the decades of corrupt neocolonial governments has made this country the poorest in the Western Hemisphere. Even prior to the January 12 earthquake, Haïti was dealing with significant challenges. Although these problems are interwoven and multifaceted, for the purpose of this study, only the economic and infrastructure challenges are addressed.

Economic Challenges

In 2009, Haïti's gross domestic product (GDP) was estimated at approximately $1,300 per capita ($6.588 billion overall).[1] The GDP is a measure of a country's overall economic output or the market value of all final goods and services made within its border in a year. The measure of the gross domestic product is often used to estimate the people's standard of living. For instance, if all the resources in Haïti were shared equitably among its citizens, each Haïtian would live on $3.54 a day. This is not much compared to a typical industrial country's GDP of $20,000 a year or $55 a day, but it would allow all Haïtians to satisfy their basic needs. Unfortunately, however, such a perfect system does not exist in Haïti or anywhere else.

As a result of greed, corruption and mismanagement, at the end of 2009, 54 percent of Haïtians were living in abject poverty or substandard conditions. In other words, this large part of the population was living without access to nutritious meals, basic health care, education or decent housing. The country depends largely on expatriates' remittances to family members. According to the Inter-American Development Bank, Haïtians abroad

> **Systematic plunder of the country's resources by the European and North American powers that colonized and occupied Haïti throughout its history and by decades of corrupt neocolonial governments has made this country the poorest in the Western Hemisphere.**

remitted $1.87 billion to their relatives in Haïti in 2008. This astounding amount made up more than 26 percent of the country's GDP. Furthermore, the Haïtian government relied on formal international economic assistance for fiscal sustainability.

Although it is difficult to measure unemployment in Haïti, the consensus among observers inside and outside of the country is that unemployment was already extremely high. The CIA's *World Factbook* notes that "more than two-thirds of the labor force does not have formal jobs."[2] Many of the hundreds of thousands of "little" merchants who jam the sidewalks and even the streets of metropolitan areas do not make enough profit to drink a bottle of cold water costing about 36 cents. To make matters worse, the economic growth Haïti had experienced from 2005 to 2008 (about 3.5 percent) was obliterated by the disastrous hurricane season of 2008. In short, Haïti's economy was already in dire condition before the calamitous earthquake.

Infrastructure Challenges

In recent years, many new roads have been built in Haïti, mostly in Port-au-Prince and in a few major cities, such as Jacmel and Cap Haïtian. However, due to lack of maintenance, the absence of proper sewage systems and obstruction of existing roads with garbage, many of these roads are full of potholes or completely destroyed. Most of the so-called "roads" in the rest of the country mirror the conditions of the Middle Ages. Any little drop of rain transforms them into lakes of mud and gravel. In addition to the terrible condition of the roads, public transportation is a nightmare. Almost any vehicle that moves carries passengers regardless of its safety condition. Pickup trucks without camper shells, 10-wheeler construction trucks, school buses without seats and broken-down cars are used as public transportation, carrying schoolchildren, merchants and factory workers. By the end of 2009, although there were two government-run companies, Dignité (Dignity) and Service Plus, using comfortable buses to provide transportation to schoolchildren and the general public at reasonable fees, they were far from having enough buses to replace the dangerous vehicles on the road.

Decent roads and safe transportation were not the only infrastructure challenges Haïti was dealing with before the January 12 murderous quake. Fewer than 30 percent of Haïtians had access to electricity, and almost half of the users illegally tapped into the national grid that ran mostly on diesel. There were longstanding problems with garbage and solid waste collection, deforestation and lack of urban planning and building codes. People built their homes or shacks anywhere, including on riverbanks or in the middle of canals. Although many beautiful hotels and beach resorts existed, there were not enough international standard hotel rooms to welcome visitors.

In Haïti a child can go to school free of charge from kindergarten to the university. Unfortunately, there are not enough state-run schools to educate the growing population. To fill this void, religious institutions and the private sector invested in education by building primary and secondary schools. Other citizens, mostly former schoolteachers with less financial means, also erected many unsafe and hazardous buildings that they called schools.

Summary of New Challenges Brought by the Earthquake

The January 12, 2010, earthquake has exacerbated all of these challenges and the precarious condition of the country. An estimated 30,000 commercial buildings as well as most of the important government buildings and landmarks, such as the National Palace, the Tax

Homeless earthquake survivors build a temporary shelter in an already crowded soccer stadium in the Santa Teresa area of Petionville, Haïti. *(Paul Jeffrey)*

Collection Central Office, the Port-au-Prince City Hall, the Port-au-Prince Cathedral and many more national landmarks were destroyed. Many schools in the capital, including the prestigious Nouveau College Bird and College Saint Louis de Gonzague, run respectively by The Methodist Church in Haïti and the Catholic Church, have become mountains of rubble. Many major roads, such as La Route Nationale 2 (National Route 2), were seriously damaged in several areas. The international airport and port in Port-au-Prince have both been damaged. About 300,000 were injured during the earthquake and needed immediate medical attention. More than a million people who became homeless are now living in ad hoc camps and tent cities that place them in grave danger during the hurricane season. These people are in need of alternative shelter, food, job, counseling and relocation before the rebuilding can start. According to a Fault Lines Al Jazeera Network report, "To clear up all the rubble in the capital, it would take 12 hours a day for an entire year, if the country had a fleet of 1,000 trucks."[3] To make matters worse, among the estimated 300,000 people who perished during the earthquake, were hundreds of professional men and women in whom the country had invested considerable resources and whose skills and capacities would have helped in the planning and rebuilding process.

New Opportunities for Haïti and Its People

The Romanized Chinese term for crisis is *wei ji*. Depending on the interpretation, these two characters respectively mean *danger* and *opportunity*. In the case of Haïti, the dangerous 7.0 magnitude earthquake that brought so much destruction and so many challenges to the country could also bring new opportunities for Haïti and its people. At the end of June 2010, the majority staff of the U.S. Senate Committee on Foreign Relations, a committee led by Senator John Kerry of

Massachusetts, issued a report, "Haïti at a Crossroads." The report's preamble affirms, "Haïti is at a significant crossroads, with limited time to enact key policies and programs that will allow the country to build a more sustainable and prosperous future."[4] This statement echoed Haïtian Prime Minister Jean-Max Bellerive's declaration, "In honor of all those who have died in this monumental tragedy, we vow to create a new Haïti that is stronger and more vibrant than ever before."[5]

> **The hope is that out of the rubble and ashes of the devastation, a new, more developed and prosperous Haïti will rise like a phoenix.**

As we have already seen, the calamitous earthquake brought an outpouring of support and promises of financial assistance to the Haïti. In addition to diverse fundraising events organized for Haïti around the world, on March 31, 2010, at the international donor conference, United Nations (U.N.) member states and international partners pledged $5.3 billion for the first 18 months to begin Haïti's reconstruction process. The total amount of pledges over three years and beyond added up to $9.9 billion. Echoing the new opportunity and hope for the Haïtian people, the United Nations General Secretary, Ban Ki-Moon said,

> As we move from emergency aid to long-term reconstruction, what we envision is a wholesale national renewal, a sweeping exercise in nation-building on a scale and scope not seen in generations. Today, we have mobilized to give Haïti and its people what they need most: hope for a new future. We have made a good start, we need now to deliver.[6]

The active involvement of former President Bill Clinton, U.N. Special Envoy to Haïti and a good friend of the country in assisting the government officials, is an encouraging factor. His love and respect for the people should be noted and emulated by others at all levels. At the donor's conference, President Clinton unambiguously stated, "My job will be to maximize the inputs and the impact of all donors—in a transparent way." He also emphasized the need for all stakeholders, most important the Haïtian people, as well as the diaspora communities and state and local governments to be included in the reconstruction process that must offer new opportunities for economic advancement for Haïtian people, specifically for women.

The hope is that out of the rubble and ashes of the devastation, a new, more developed and prosperous Haïti will rise like a phoenix.[7] There is indeed hope for better days for Haïti and its people, because the potential to rebuild a better and more sustainable country is within reach. This will happen provided that the donor countries and institutions follow through with their pledges and that all Haïtians, inside and outside of the country, work together with Haïti's friends. The Haïtian authorities must also seize the moment and undertake bold actions to make this a defining time in the economic and social development of the nation.

Notes

1. Central Intelligence Agency (CIA) *World Factbook*, http://www.cia.gog/the-world-factbook (accessed September 25, 2010).
2. Ibid.
3. Avi Lewis, "The Politics of Rebuilding," Fault Lines, Al Jazeera, January 29, 2010, http://english.aljazeera.net/programmes/faultlines/2010/02/201021113542380300.html.

4. The full report can be accessed from the committee website at http://foreign.senate.gov/.
5. See Jan-Max Bellerive, "Vowing to Build a Prosperous Future for Haiti," February 1, 2010, http://www.huffingtonpost.com/jeanmax-bellerive/vowing-to-build-a-prosper_b_444353.html.
6. See International Donors Conference Toward a New Future for Haiti, [home page], http://www.haiticonference.org (accessed September 25, 2010).
7. In ancient mythology, the phoenix was a bird resembling an eagle that lived for 500 years and then burned itself to death on a pyre from whose ashes another phoenix arose. It is sometimes used as a symbol of death and resurrection.

Novembre Simon, 35, carries a small pine tree for replanting as part of a reforestation project in the mountainous community of Foret-des-Pins, Haïti. Plagued by deforestation, much of it to produce charcoal for urban cooking stoves, she and other residents of the area are volunteering to work with the Lutheran World Federation and International Orthodox Christian Charities to reforest and protect their environment. *(Paul Jeffrey)*

Epilogue
Hopes and Dreams for Haïti and Its People

In the year that over 300,000 of my sisters and brothers suddenly went to sleep with their African ancestors, I was sitting alone on a porch 681 miles and a 90-minute flight away from the mountains of rubble and the smelly smoke of burning bodies and rubbish, lamenting the plight of my homeland and of its people. I felt inadequate and powerless before such horrible human loss and devastation. As lament gave way to meditation, prayer and quietness, I was transported to a green prairie where healthy and happy children were playing, giggling, singing, telling and listening to stories their parents had once told them. They were mahogany, milk chocolate, dark chocolate and peach shades of boys and girls. All had clean clothes, pretty shoes and seemed to be well-fed. From a distance, I saw many majestic mountains covered with all kinds of trees. Some of the trees had big red, yellow and white flowers. Some had fruits hanging high and low on their branches, and others were there just to give shade and protect the land against erosion. Everything was so beautiful. I was in awe and exclaimed, "Oh my God! Where am I?"

Then I heard a sweet and melodious voice, full of grace and tenderness, answer, "Did you call me, son?" The being was strange and unfamiliar to me, but I was not afraid, for her voice was as calming as a gentle afternoon breeze. She appeared to be seated on a throne and her long, colorful and silky robe covered the entire seat. She had six hands; with two she covered her face to prevent me from seeing her clearly, with two she covered her feet and with two she flew. I noticed she was of a beautiful dark brown shade and had short and dark hair similar to that of some of the children. As soon as the little ones saw her, they stopped what they were doing, formed a circle around her and began singing:

Holy! Holy! Holy!
Holy is the mother of the world.
This land has been blessed,
It has been revived, because of your love
And of your generous children
Here, there and everywhere.
Holy! Holy! Holy!
Holy is the mother of the world.

I inquired, "Who are you, holy one?" She replied, "I am the one whom you called and asked, 'Where am I?'" The creature continued and said, "Come with me." She lifted me gently with one hand and flew with me to the top of the highest mountain. I felt so good in the company of the "mother," as if I had known her all my life. I felt safe and protected near her. We were flying high, higher than the birds of the air, higher than the clouds in the sky. Yet I feared no danger. I was confident and at peace. Suddenly, this song I learned as a child came to my mind and I was humming:

Always joyful, this is our pledge;
Joyful of having Jesus Christ as Savior.
Yes, joyful even when we are despised,
Nothing could sadden our heart.
Do not fear the adversary,
Let's walk as we sing to heaven.
Already Triumphant on earth,
Always joyful, always joyful.[1]
(Repeat last three lines)

[handwritten note: Maybe put to my own music.]

The beautiful and loving creature put me down gently and commanded, "Look into the plains and the valleys and tell me what you see!" I saw lots of people moving about as though they were working, but I could not distinguish them or what they were doing. I said, "My mother, I can see everything is beautiful, but I cannot identify what they are or what they are doing." With her index finger, the creature touched my eyes and said, "Now that I have touched you, your guilt, your sadness and frustration, as well as your sense of powerlessness are departed and you are made whole again. Open your eyes and tell me now what you see."

Behold, I looked and saw beautiful hotels and restaurants, not only in the capital but also at every corner of the land. Thousands and thousands of people, yellow people, light brown people, pink people and dark brown people from the entire known and unknown world, leaving from and going into the hotels and restaurants. I also saw stores, big and small, filled with goods, and local people also had money to buy from them. I saw colorful *tap taps*[2] that looked like art displays. I also saw autobuses, ferry boats, trains, scooters and bicycles carrying students and workers to school and to work, to the beaches, to museums and to the parks. There were no traffic jams because private cars were not allowed in the cities between the hours of 6 a.m. and 6 p.m.

There were enough schools for all of the children and colleges, universities and technical schools for the young people and the adults. I saw clean and spacious apartment buildings and single-family houses. No one was living in shacks or on the streets. Mentally challenged people and older adults were cared for in special facilities conducive to their needs. Each neighborhood had a well-equipped and staffed hospital or medical clinic. I also saw farmers returning to their lands and utilizing appropriate tools and resources to work and harvest the bounty from their land. All had enough food to eat and to sell. When I looked in the valleys, I saw clean rivers flowing freely and with abundant water because there were trees everywhere to protect them. The beaches, even the public ones, were clean and had shades and toilets. They were filled with young and old lovers coming hand in hand to watch the sunset and enjoy the afternoon breeze. Some were taking pictures, others were kissing and talking softly and some were just standing still and contemplating the natural beauty of the land.

Technologies were not used against nature, but the two combined for the benefit of the people. There were windmills in every city and village and solar panels on top of every building to produce electricity and cooking energy. All the streets were paved and clean. Garbage and solid waste were collected periodically and on time. Some was recycled to make other useful products, and some was transformed into compost to make natural gas and fertilizer. Nothing was lost, wasted, or left unattended.

As I was admiring the beauty of the land, the sustainability of its economy, the ingenuity and the joy of its people, I wondered in my heart, "What kind of leaders must these people have to produce such a result?" Though I was not speaking, the "mother" heard my thoughts and could even see my most secret desires. She answered, "They are ordinary local people governing themselves and managing the country's resources for the benefit of the people who are living in the land now and that of the future generations." After that, she said, "Come closer and see." She flew down to the plains and valleys with me and took me inside the government buildings. There I saw qualified professional women and men working efficiently on behalf of the people. I also saw civil servants refusing to take bribes or kickbacks in exchange for their service. Furthermore, I saw no one was above the law, and justice was rendered equitably and swiftly.

I was dumbfounded by what I saw and softly asked the "mother," "Has this land always been that beautiful and well organized with justice and equity?" The way she smiled made me realize the naïveté of my inquiry. But instead of rebuking me for my ignorance, she showed me a desolated land filled with rubble and piles of trash, a land where people slept under makeshift tents and said, "This was the land before its transformation, for nothing is impossible with me and for those who believe in me."

Looking at the land before its present condition, I was perplexed and asked with supplication, "Mother, please tell me, where am I?" With a sweet but firm voice that echoed in my ears, she responded, "This is your transformed and liberated native land after the awful disaster." Then she said, "I need my children to accompany the people in their quest for liberation and justice. I need my children to make this transformation happen, whom shall I send, and who will go for us?" I responded, "Here I am, Mother, send me." She said, "Go and tell my people: keep listening and comprehend, keep looking and understand. There is hope for their land. It will be transformed with my grace and the help of my children."

As I was about to ask another question, I heard my youngest son say, "Jep, why are you smiling in your sleep? Whatever you might be dreaming about must be good because it made you happy. I prayed that God will make your dreams come true."

"It will be. It will come true with God's grace," I replied, still smiling.

Notes

1. The author's translation of a verse of the French song *"Toujours Joyeux"* ("Always Joyful") from the "Melodies Joyeuses" in *Les Chants D'Esperance* (Port-au-Prince, Haïti: La Presse Evangélique, 1995), 162.
2. Tap taps are trucks with a camper shell, built locally by Haïtian carpenters and beautifully decorated by Haïtian artists. Some tap taps are transformed into mini vans.

Now it's your turn. You are invited to prayerfully share your dreams and hopes for Haïti and its people in the pages that follow.

My Hopes and Dreams for Haïti

Immediate (Healing) physical & eternal spiritual needs met.
Restored infrastructure
Just leaders who empower the citizens.
Salvation - WOG preached, taught, & accepted.

Rev. 21 & Selected verses of Micah.

In addition to praying daily for my brothers and sisters in Haïti, I will do the following to help fulfill my hope and dreams for Haïti:

- Continue to prepare & research problems/solutions
- Teach class & teach beyond to empower others.
- Pray for myself & more compassion/love/wisdom.

I will find out what God wants to do & empower others to do it by...

compassionate Christian mission / not only a service organization

My Hopes and Dreams for Haïti

In addition to praying daily for my brothers and sisters in Haïti, I will do the following to help fulfill my hope and dreams for Haïti:

Students at the Notre Dame de Petits school at the beginning of a school day in Port-au-Prince, Haïti. The school's building collapsed in the January 2010 earthquake, and while some classes are conducted in the ruins, other classes meet in large tents provided by International Orthodox Christian Charities. *(Paul Jeffrey)*

Bibliography

"12 Janvier 2010: Tremblement de Terre" ["January 12, 2010: Earthquake"]. *Le Nouveliste* (Special edition, January–February 2010).

August, G. D. *Histoire de Mon Pays, Haïti*, 2ème édition [*History of My Country, Haïti*. 2nd edition]. Port-au-Prince: Henri Deschamps, 1993.

Boff, Leonardo. *Jesus Christ Liberator: A Critical Christology for Our Time*. Maryknoll, N.Y.: Orbis Books, 1984.

Boff, Leonardo, and Boff, Clodovis. *Introducing Liberation Theology*. Maryknoll, N.Y.: Orbis Books, 1987.

Brown, Robert McAfee. *Liberation Theology: An Introductory Guide*. Louisville, Ky.: Westminster/John Knox Press, 1993.

Casséus, Jules. *Haïti: Quelle Èglise . . . Quelle Liberation?* [*Haïti: What Kind of Church . . . What Kind of Freedom?*]. Miami, Fla.: The Little River Press, 1991.

Central Intelligence Agency. *World Factbook*. 2009. Available: https://www.cia.gov/the-world-factbook.

Chants d'Esperance [Songs of Hope], 5th edition. Port-au-Prince: La Presse Evangélique, 1995.

Chomsky, Noam. *Year 501: The Conquest Continues*. Boston: South End Press, 1993.

Cone, James H. *God of the Oppressed*. Maryknoll, N.Y.: Orbis Books, 1997.

Davenport, Gene L. *Into the Darkness*. Nashville: Abingdon Press, 1988.

De Marco, Jenna. "Groups Begin Preliminary Work for Long-term Recovery in Haïti," 1178 E-review, Florida Annual Conference, June 3, 2010.

Dorsainvil, J. C. *Histoire d'Haïti: Cours Secondaire* [*History of Haïti: Secondary Level*]. Edition No. PDHG 129. Port-au-Prince: Henri Deschands, 1987.

Farmer, Paul. *The Uses of Haïti*. Monroe, Maine: Common Courage Press, 2006.

Fern, Deane William. *Third World Liberation Theologies: An Introductory Survey*. Maryknoll, N.Y.: Orbis Books, 1988.

Fouchard, Jean. *Les Marrons de la Liberté*. Paris, France: Edition de l'École, 1972.

Griffiths, Leslie J. *A History of Methodism in Haïti*. Port-au-Prince: Imprimerie Méthodiste–D.E.L., 1986.

Gutiérrez, Gustavo. *A Theology of Liberation: History, Politics and Salvation*. Maryknoll, N.Y.: Orbis Books, 1973.

Hanke, Lewis. *The Spanish Struggle for Justice in the Conquest of America*. Boston: Little Brown & Company, 1966.

Hoffman, Léon-François. *Haïti: Couleurs, Croyances, Créole* [*Haïti: Color, Beliefs, Creole*]. Montreal, Québec: CIDIHCA; Port-au-Prince: Editions Henri Deschamps, 1990.

Johnson, Garrett. "Lessons from Another Forgotten American Occupation." *Bits of News*, April 24, 2008. Available: http://www.bitsofnews.com/content/view/8108/.

Katz, Jonathan M. "Clinton: Donors Still Holding Out on Haïti Pledges." The Associated Press (August 6, 2010). Available : http://www.boston.com/news/world/latinamerica/articles/2010/08/06/clinton_donors_still_holding_out_on_haiti_pledges/.

Kristoff, Madeline and Liz Panarelli. "Haïti: A Republic of NGOs?" April 2010. Available: http://www.usip.org/programs/initiatives/Haiti-working-group.

"La Dette de la France à Haïti," ["France's Debt to Haïti"]. *Haïti Progrès* 12, no. 31 (October 15–21, 2003).

Laguerre, Michel S. *The Military and Society in Haïti*. Knoxville: University of Tennessee Press, 1993.

Neibuhr, H. Richard. *Christ and Culture*. New York: Harper Collins, 1996.

Ridgeway, James. *The Haïti Files: Decoding the Crisis*. Washington, D.C.: Essential Books/Azul Editions, 1994.

Sifflet, Jason. "Haïti Didn't Jump, It Was Pushed!" *St. Lucia Star*, March 15, 2010. Available: http://stluciastar.com/content/archives/11745/comment-page-1.

Spink, Kathryn. *Mother Teresa: A Complete Authorized Biography*. San Francisco: HarperSanFrancisco, 1997.

Turnier, Alain. *Quand la Nation Demande des Comptes* [*When the Nation Asks for Accountability*]. Port-au-Prince: Editions Le Natal, 1989.

United States Senate Committee on Foreign Relations. "Haïti at a Crossroads," June 22, 2010: U.S. Government Printing Office, 2010. Available: http://foreign.senate.gov/.

Wilentz, Amy. *The Rainy Season : Haïti Since Duvalier*. New York: Simon and Schuster, 1989.

Additional Web Resources

United Methodist Women
www.unitedmethodistwomen.org

General Board of Global Ministries of The United Methodist Church
www.gbgm-umc.org

Florida Annual Conference of The United Methodist Church
www.flumc.org

Haïti Earthquake Relief and Recovery, William J. Clinton Foundation
www.clintonfoundation.org/haiti_longstanding/haiti_earthquakerecovery.php

Haïtian Artisans for Peace International
www.haitianartisans.com

"Haïti's History of Misery," BBC News
news.bbc.co.uk/2/hi/americas/8456728.stm

International Donors Conference Toward a New Future for Haïti
www.haiticonference.org

Michigan Area Haïti Task Force
www.stovern.net/Haiti

OneResponse
www.oneresponse.info/Disasters/Haiti

"The Politics of Rebuilding," *Fault Lines*, Al Jazeera
english.aljazeera.net/programmes/faultlines/2010/02/201021113542380300.html

"Rebuilding Haïti," *Fault Lines*, Al Jazeera
english.aljazeera.net/news/americas/2010/01/20101252235137354.html

Tainos Caribs
www.kwabs.com/tainos_caribs.html

A homeless earthquake survivor builds a temporary shelter in an already crowded soccer stadium in the Santa Teresa area of Petionville, Haïti. *(Paul Jeffrey)*

Study Leader's Guide
By Dr. M. René Johnson

Introduction

Haïti is a land of contrasts, rich in culture—a blend of Spanish, French, African and indigenous influences—and rich in spirit. Haïti faces enormous challenges, yet amid the devastation from the earthquake are glimmers of hope. When confronted with such stark contrasts between the beauty of its people and the ugliness of its crushing poverty, we can fall into oversimplified perspectives of what is wrong with Haïti and what will set things right.

Our inclination as Christians is to reach out in love. How can we be of help? Likewise, following the earthquake, the instinct of many people was to help by donating money. United States citizens are "take charge" sorts of people. Is there a problem? Let's solve it. Is something broken? Let's fix it. Collectively, we like to jump in, get down to business and tackle the impossible, but we can also be impatient. The people of the United States are results oriented, and so the obstacles that hampered relief efforts in Haïti following the earthquake understandably frustrated many of us. Supplies of food, water and medicines initially sat idle in the staging area. Roads were clogged. People and vehicles couldn't get in or out of Port-au-Prince. It was heartbreaking to see people in such desperate need with relief supplies so close by and yet seemingly unreachable.

Wanting to help is a good thing. Jesus told us to "Give to everyone who asks you" (Luke 6:30, NIV). Generosity is a Christian response to having received generously from God. Sadly, so much of our giving comes with strings attached or only to people we decide are "deserving." Jesus, however, wants us to give as God gives. Jesus also told the rich young man to "Go, sell everything you have and give to the poor" (Mark 10:21, NIV). Again, such generosity goes beyond our usual understanding of charity. Jesus insists that the rich need to be in solidarity with the poor. But the history of Christian mission is one in which Christians haven't always given what was needed—hair curlers to women in Africa is but one incredulous example (the Rev. Lynn DeMoss of West Michigan Conference, a former missionary to the Democratic Republic of Congo, "Like Star Wars, Mission Has Its Dark Side," Saginaw Bay District United Methodist Women Spiritual Life Retreat, May 1–2, 2009). So although the command is simple and clear—*give*—how best to respond to needs can be complicated and unclear. We need and want to give, but Christians also need to give thoughtfully and effectively.

Two questions, among many, that Christians should reflect on are "How can the church be in mission *with* the people of Haïti rather than in mission *to*?" and "How do we relinquish positions of power in order to be in partnership with the people of Haïti?" These are questions of discernment that will assist us in figuring out how best to respond to helping the Haïtian people meet their needs because it matters how we go about doing God's business. How we give to others can potentially foster the recipient's dependence on charity, or our gifts can become a means for recipients to develop and enhance their gifts and abilities to provide for themselves.

This study provides support to Christians who desire to help the people of Haïti by offering readers opportunity to learn more about Haïti, reflect theologically on the command to be in mission, pray for wisdom in discerning how to be of help and ultimately to act in love.

Goals and Objectives

The goal of this study is to inform Christians about the situation in Haïti so that mission work there will be aligned with Christ's vision of the kingdom of God. As the previous section points out, however, even when Christians can agree on a goal—such as bringing about the kingdom of God—finding the path to achieve the goal can be difficult. Just as there are potentially several routes one might take to drive from one place to another, there are potentially different routes that study classes can take to reach this goal. This is but one option to help you map out your direction. Although you may have additional objectives for the study you lead, these three are essential:

- To provide sufficient background on Haïti's history and culture to understand the current challenges the people of Haïti face.

- To learn about the theology that informs the church's mission work in Haïti.

- To learn ways in which individuals and church groups can support the recovery efforts in Haïti.

In each session of this study guide, these objectives, or similar ones, will be reinforced by repeating a consistent process: learning, reflecting and finding ways to act.

Methods

Because this is a mission study, you want participants to learn more about Haïti, but don't lose sight of the other aspects of teaching. You are doing more than dispensing information. Be mindful of people's emotional, spiritual, social and physical needs as you plan. Images of poverty and the death and destruction following the January 2010 earthquake can evoke strong feelings of anger and sadness. The scale of the earthquake and loss of life can lead to a spiritual crisis. At some point in our faith journeys, we confront evil and injustice and must find an answer to the question "Why do bad things happen to innocent people?" As study leader, you may need to guide participants through that troubling question.

You could certainly refer them to Rabbi Harold Kushner's classic book on the subject, *When Bad Things Happen to Good People*. Also remind them of the numerous scriptures that assure us of God's promise to be present with us regardless of what happens (the 23rd Psalm, for example).

Don't be tempted to omit worship segments during your study time in favor of packing more reading and discussion into your sessions. This is not only a *school* of mission; it is a school of *Christian* mission. Issues of oppression, injustice and the destruction from the earthquake need to be tied to our understanding of God, and it is unfortunate that the media tends to pick up primarily on the faulty theology of "blame the victim" or "the earthquake is God's punishment." Litanies, scriptures, prayers and hymns can all assist in putting Haïti's history, culture and challenges into proper perspective and can lead participants to respond in ways that affirm our faith in a just and loving God.

Be hospitable. Provide beverages and snacks if possible. Allow break time for people to stand and move. No one wants to sit still for hours on end. Find a blend of time for listening to a speaker with time for group discussion or other activities. Remember, too, that hospitality means starting and ending at the posted times. The study guide provides a time frame to help you pace the amount of time spent on each activity or segment. They are, however, only suggestions. Each group will approach the material a bit differently. One class may race through an activity while another group will need additional time. Give yourself some latitude to adjust the schedule to meet the unique needs of your class.

Adults learn in different ways. Some learn best by listening and taking notes. Others learn best by seeing, whether pictures, objects or words on a poster. Yet others will retain information better if they do something with their hands—thumb through the book to find information, physically write ideas down on paper or engage in a craft. Music and singing engage people in ways the written word cannot. (How often is music the highlight of a worship service for you?) You may prefer one particular mode of learning for yourself—this guide relies heavily, for example, on reading and reflection because of my years of teaching college writing courses—but try to provide a variety of methods so participants can find a way into the material that is meaningful to them. These session plans are a guide map only. Lead your class through the material drawing from your strengths and their styles.

Preparing to Lead

Developing a Mission Study Team
Who can help you with planning and leading the study? Who could lead music? Do you know someone who has been on a mission trip to Haïti? Does someone have a flair for setting up table displays? Don't try to go it alone. Although it is important to have one person in charge to oversee the process and coordinate efforts, it is equally important to work as a team and delegate responsibilities. As you develop a team, consider new people you could draw into participation—strive for diversity.

Determining the Time and Space
Will you be able to offer four sessions to cover the study thoroughly, or will you be able to devote only an hour or so? What day of the week and what time of day will be convenient for people to attend? Retirees may prefer a late morning or early afternoon, but people who work may prefer an evening or weekend. Check what other activities and events are planned in your community. Will you be competing against a major event? Can you tap into a compatible community event to promote your study? How many people do you expect to attend? Find an appropriately sized space. If you plan to use video, make sure you can control the light, depending on the time of day. Will the space accommodate the configuration you want? Do you need round tables to encourage small group discussion? Do you need seating for participants to face an invited speaker at a podium? If your event is longer than an hour, how comfortable are the chairs? If people will likely take notes, will the seating allow them a surface to write?

Publicizing Your Event
Who will attend? Are you planning exclusively for members of your local United Methodist Women unit? Or are you planning to include all adults in your church congregation? If you plan to invite others in your community to learn about Haïti, how will you reach them? Is there another congregation that would be interested in co-sponsoring an event? Check with the pastor at your church if your town has a ministerial board. Another option is to collaborate with the United Methodist Women units in your cluster, or shepherding, group. Use a variety of modes of communication—church newsletter, posters or flyers and your church's website if you have one.

What You Need
The most obvious need is the study book, but you may want to consider whether books are essential for every study participant. The ideal situation is, of course, one in which every participant not only has a copy of the study but has also read it cover to cover before the first study session begins. Realistically, some participants may have purchased the book already but haven't yet read it, and many participants may not even have a copy. The session activities have been designed to accommodate participants who haven't read the text. Those who have read the text are further ahead, but the activities

Haïti: Challenges and Hope | 71

will help them reflect on the material more deeply. Because some activities rely on small groups reading and gleaning information from sections of the study book, if participants aren't required to purchase a copy, you will need three to five copies for the classroom.

Once you have determined the space for the study, you can turn your attention to the supplies you'll need. You can be as low-tech or high-tech in your approach as you desire. Depending on the classroom, you may want to use a chalkboard or whiteboard with markers, a large-format newsprint pad of paper, notebook paper with pens or pencils, or a laptop with projector if you're tech-savvy. Just bear in mind that even when using Power-Point, class participants will need paper to take notes or complete small group activities. As always, you need to be prepared for technological glitches. Projector bulbs do burn out occasionally, so if a replacement bulb isn't available, you need to be flexible enough to switch to "Plan B" at a moment's notice. Even low-tech materials need to be checked ahead of time. Markers dry out, and pencils need to be sharpened. Because worship is a significant part of each session, consider whether you will need a CD player for music or whether you need to arrange for someone to play piano. Note that the worship segments make extensive use of *The United Methodist Hymnal (UMH)* (Nashville: The United Methodist Publishing House, 1989) and *The Faith We Sing (TFWS)* (Nashville: Abingdon Press, 2000). Sources of other music are also identified.

Single-session Option (One Hour)

Introduction

Encouraging people to commit to a longer, more in-depth study of Haïti is preferable, but given the reality of people's schedules, you may be able to devote only an hour to covering the study in a United Methodist Women's unit meeting, mission sampler event or adult Sunday school class. Resist the temptation to try to cover everything. People can absorb only so much information at a time, so follow the advice of the truism "Less is more." Participants will gain more from a session that limits its focus than one that covers everything in "fast forward" mode.

Objectives

The primary purpose of this session is to introduce participants to the study book and provide a simple structure—Haïti's past, present and future—to help them answer two basic questions people ask regarding Haïti: "Why is Haïti so poor?" and "What can I do to help?" To accomplish this goal, the class will focus on three objectives:

- To understand the impact of colonialism on Haïti.

- To learn about the current challenges the people of Haïti face.

- To discover ways in which we can support recovery efforts in Haïti.

For this session, you will need hymnals; a chalkboard, whiteboard, or large pad of newsprint; markers; three copies of the study book (one for each of the small groups if you don't expect participants to have bought personal copies); index cards; pens or pencils; and handouts of the worship service. When you set up the room, be sure to include a worship center. You will need to include a small offering plate or basket for the commitment cards that participants will fill out for the closing worship.

Opening Worship (5 minutes)

Greeting

Leader: *Sak pase* [Sack pah-see]? What's up?

People: We are here to learn about the people of Haïti, their history and their culture. We are here because we want to respond to the challenges the people of Haïti face. We will listen to stories of FAITH. We will express HOPE for the future. Then we will put LOVE IN ACTION so that our faith will prove our hope true.

Song: "When We Are Called to Sing Your Praise," TFWS #2216

Responsive Scripture Reading: Psalm 46:1-3, 7 (NIV)

Leader: God is our refuge and strength,
All: **an ever-present help in trouble.**
Leader: Therefore we will not fear, though the earth give way
All: **and the mountains fall into the heart of the sea,**
Leader: though its waters roar and foam
All: **and the mountains quake with their surging.**
Leader: The Lord Almighty is with us;
All: **the God of Jacob is our fortress.**

Prayer

Gracious and loving God, you are always faithful to your people. When our faith falters in the face of tragedy, surround us with the comfort of your Holy Spirit and grant us courage to meet the challenges of each

Haïti: Challenges and Hope | 73

day. As we grapple with Haïti's painful past and the enormity of Haïti's present burden to rebuild, fill our hearts with your compassion that we might join hands with our brothers and sisters to lighten their load. In the name of your Son who said, "My yoke is easy and my burden is light." Amen.

Activity: Starting with Stereotypes (5 minutes)

Do a shout-out to gain a sense of what participants know about Haïti. Ask them for words or short phrases that describe Haïti and its people. Record the group's responses on a pad of newsprint or a chalkboard. Expect to hear answers that reflect negative images, such as "poverty-stricken," "illiterate," and "voodoo." Don't debate the responses at this time. Encourage short answers from as many participants as possible. Assure participants that there will be time to reflect on and discuss the words after you have compiled a sufficient list.

When the group has exhausted ideas for the list, ask the group where they learned this information. Most participants will likely indicate television and perhaps newspaper or magazine articles, while others will have utilized websites. Some may actually have firsthand knowledge of Haïti. As an addition or an alternative, you could provide magazines and newspaper clippings with photographs for the class to examine for stereotypes. Remind everyone that what we see in the media is only a small glimpse of Haïti and that the purpose of the study is to increase our knowledge and understanding, but it too is only an introduction.

Caution participants that what they may learn about the colonial and not-so-distant past may cause uncomfortable feelings—shame and anger, for example, or denial of our country's part in oppressing the Haïtian people. We need to keep open minds in order to learn. Theologically, this means confessing our sin and repenting so that our present and future interactions with the people of Haïti will reflect God's love.

Ask participants what they most want to learn about Haïti or what issues interest them most. Let them know what you will be able to cover in the session and point them to resources for further study. If interest is sufficient, you may be able to offer a follow-up study. In this session you will briefly examine Haïti's past, present and future—a tall order!

Learn: Small Group Activity (25 minutes)

Divide the class into three groups. Group 1 will focus on Haïti's past, especially addressing the question "Why is Haïti so poor?" This group will report on the reasons for Haïti's poverty by examining its history. This group will review Chapter 1 in the study book. Suggest that the group record the names of the colonial powers that ruled Haïti in the past and then list what they gained or took from Haïti while in another column they list what the colonial powers gave or contributed to Haïti. In short, the group will provide a "balance sheet" of sorts, weighing the positive and negative impacts of each colonial power.

Group 2's assignment is to make a list of Haïti's present challenges. This group will review Chapter 3 and Chapter 5 through the section "Summary of New Challenges Brought by the Earthquake." This group will focus on answering the question "What needs to be done to rebuild Haïti?" In addition to literal rebuilding, suggest that the group also include what needs to be done to help people rebuild emotionally, socially and spiritually.

Group 3 will look to Haïti's future. This group will focus on the question "What can we do?" Increasing our knowledge about Haïti is an admirable goal, but the pursuit of knowledge for its own sake is not the ultimate goal of this study. In regard to Haïti, the hope is that increased knowledge will lead to more effective mission efforts. To that end, Group 3 will consider what Christians can do collectively as the church as well as what we can do individually. Helpful sections of the study for this group to review are Chapter 4, the "New Opportunities for Haïti and Its People" section of Chapter 5 and the Epilogue.

Reflect (20 minutes)

Allot each group three to five minutes to report back to the class as a whole. Then have participants reflect on the following questions:

- What resources does Haïti have to overcome its challenges?

- What resources do I have that I could share with Haïti's people?

Closing Worship (5 minutes)

Song: "Halle, Halle, Halleluja," TFWS #2026

Act of Commitment

Give participants an index card or small sheet of paper (cut standard size copy paper into quarters) and ask them to write down one action they can take to assist the people of Haïti. When everyone has written down an act of love on behalf of Haïti, participants should place their commitment cards in an offering plate or basket. Then offer the following prayer as a consecration of the gifts of service.

Closing Prayer

We thank you, God, for all the blessings you have given us. You challenge us to follow your way, and so we ask you to open our minds to hear your word and give us hearts of love that we might share what we have with those who have little. Open our eyes, Lord, to see opportunities to be in mission to the world, and open our souls to the promptings of your spirit. All this we pray in the name of the one who came to be servant of all. Amen.

Song: "Faith, While Trees Are Still in Blossom," UMH #508

Alternate Options for a One-Session Event

Haïti Worship Service

If you have an opportunity to invite a speaker who has been on a mission trip to Haïti, you may want to develop your session as an hour-long worship service with the speaker's message in place of a sermon. Pull together appropriate music, Scripture readings, litanies and prayers from the four sessions that follow. Provide a fellowship time afterward for attendees to ask questions and meet the speaker.

Haïti Mission Fair

You may want to set up tables or displays for a mission fair event. Have a room or area set aside to show videos of Haïti, or put together a slideshow of photographs from mission trips that members of your church have taken. Set up a series of tables that participants can navigate easily. Design poster boards with basic information about Haïti's geography, climate and population facts. Then put together displays with information about UMCOR and UMVIM and offer brochures or flyers for upcoming mission trips sponsored by your district or annual conference. You may also want to set up an area where people can engage in craft projects or assemble health kits or school kits, or you could offer people a taste of Haïti with foods from the Caribbean. Mission fairs provide a festive atmosphere and provide attendees with options for moving through displays at their own pace. In addition, fairs are ideal intergenerational events.

Four-session Option
(Two-hour sessions)

Session 1: The Legacy of History and Culture

Introduction

The past is prologue. We carry the past with us in the present, and so Session 1 will examine Haïti's past to provide a broad context for participants to understand why things are the way they are in Haïti. The hope of studying history is that by understanding more clearly how a situation came to be, we gain insights into how we can alter the future by making different decisions and pursuing alternate paths. We cannot change the past, and so we sometimes believe that because the past is set in stone, the future must be too. Christians, however, should not view the future with fatalism. The Bible tells us that all things are possible for God. By the same token, although we may not be able to predict the future, it is certainly within our power to influence it. A modest goal of this session, therefore, is to learn from the past so that we won't repeat its mistakes.

Objectives

Learning often requires self-examination alongside the accumulation of information, so the objectives of this session begin with self-discovery and subsequently use insights to shed light on Haïti's history and the origins of the church at Pentecost:

- To uncover personal assumptions and misconceptions about Haïti.
- To learn about the intersection of cultures that shaped Haïti's past.
- To affirm the culturally diverse nature of the church at its beginnings.

What you need for this session are hymnals, a Bible, the usual supplies of paper and pencils, a world globe and string and a "pie" made of poster board or heavy paper.

Opening Worship (10 minutes)

Greeting

Leader: *Sak pase* [Sack pah-see]? What's up?
People: **We are here to learn about the people of Haïti, their history and their culture. We are here because we want to respond to the challenges the people of Haïti face. We will listen to stories of FAITH. We will express HOPE for the future. Then we will put LOVE IN ACTION so that our faith will prove our hope true.**

Scripture: Psalm 117

Song: "From All That Dwell Below the Skies," UMH #101

Litany

Leader: Our God is God of all the nations.
People: **Our Lord is Lord of all the peoples.**
Leader: At his birth, Christ was adored by wise ones from the East.
People: **At his birth, Christ was revealed to humble shepherds.**
Leader: Christ's first followers were simple fishermen from Galilee.
People: **Christ's first followers were peasants and sinners.**
Leader: At Pentecost, Christ's followers included foreigners who spoke many languages.
People: **At Pentecost, Christ's church broke through the barriers of language and culture.**
All: **Christ's good news belongs to all peoples at all times.**

Song: "In Christ There Is No East or West,"
UMH #548

Participant Introductions (15 minutes)

Even if you are certain that everyone in the study class knows one another, reserve time for introductions. Use this opportunity to focus on cultural diversity by asking participants to tell where their ancestors came from instead of the usual information people provide about themselves. Most of us have either a multinational, multiethnic, or multiracial heritage. Jot down the names of all the countries that participants' ancestors came from on a chalkboard, or ask everyone to write their names on slips of paper and pin them on a world map. Participants' mix of heritages will provide a useful way to launch into learning about Haïti's multicultural background. Let participants know that they will use their personal histories and background to help them reflect on the diverse cultural influences that shape the Haïtian experience.

Activity: Starting with Stereotypes (15 minutes)

Ask participants to share the stereotypes they have heard about the ethnic groups that make up their heritage. What characteristics do we attribute to the British? Irish? Germans? Italians? Polish? What characteristics do we assign to Arabs? Chinese? Indians? How many of those stereotypes are positive? How many are negative? How many are accurate?

After the group has explored a number of stereotypes of nationalities, especially European nations, turn their attention to Haïti. Do the shout-out exercise explained in the Single-Session Option (see p. 74). After recording the group's responses on a pad of newsprint or a chalkboard, have the class compare stereotypes of Haïtians with the other nationalities. How well or poorly do the various nations stack up against one another? Which countries, if any, have the most favorable stereotypes? Which have the most negative ones? This exercise is not meant to pass judgment. There is no need to lecture the class about stereotypes. Maintain an atmosphere of open inquiry. The primary goal is simply to make observations rather than draw specific conclusions at this point.

When the group has wrapped up its observations about national stereotypes, shift their attention to the sources of those stereotypes. Ask participants what role the media plays in maintaining stereotypes. Ask participants what role their parents or other mentors played in transmitting attitudes. Ask them what personal experiences have shaped their attitudes. Allow some time for a few participants to share stories with the class. Remind them that self-awareness is important in general when we are engaged in learning and that keeping an open mind is a hallmark of being a United Methodist. With awareness of the prejudices participants have been exposed to throughout their lives, the class will next take a closer look at Haïti's history.

Learn: Haïti's Cultural Diversity— Then (15 minutes)

Divide participants into five groups. Assign each group a culture—Arawak, Spanish, French, African and American—and direct them to read the appropriate section from Chapter 1. Groups can supplement the information from the chapter with events on the Selected Timeline of Key Events in Haïti (see p. 7). Groups should compile a list of each culture's contributions as well as its negative impact on the indigenous people. Have each group briefly report their findings back to the whole class. You can either record their findings on a whiteboard or newsprint pad for the class or have the groups post their findings on a wall so everyone will have access to the contributions and negative impacts of each culture as participants reflect on Haïti's history.

Break (5 minutes)

Learn: Haïti's Colonial Legacy—Then and Now (15 minutes)

You will need to do some calculations for this next exercise. On the board, write the following words: "Les Blancs," "Affranchis," and "Slaves." Have the class turn to the last section of Chapter 1, "Overview of Haïti's Socioeconomic Structure," to fill in information about these groups during the colonial era. Who, in terms of race or nationality, comprises these groups? What percentage of the population is comprised of each group? Ask the class to stand in a circle, and then divide them into three groups according to the percentages: Whites, 8 percent; Mulattos, 5 percent; and African, 87 percent. If you have 25 participants, for example, two people would stand together in the circle representing Whites, one person would stand alone in the circle representing the Mulattos and 22 would represent Africans.

Now "shift" the groups to reflect the current socioeconomic class composition of Haïti: 2 percent upper class, 5 percent middle class and 93 percent the masses. In a classroom of 25 participants, this translates to one person to represent the upper class, one person in the middle class and 23 the lower class of peasants. Ask the class to identify the dominant racial composition of each economic class. It should be obvious that only a minor shift was needed. Now divide a "pie" and give each group their piece. The upper and middle class groups together receive slightly less than half of the pie. According to 2009 statistics from the CIA *World Factbook* (access the CIA's *World Factbook* online at www.cia.gov/the-world-factbook.), the top 10 percent of Haïti's population held nearly 48 percent of the income. Now divide the remaining 90 percent of the population, representing the lower class, into a group of approximately 80 percent and 10 percent. In this hypothetical classroom, that means divide the group of 23 into a group of 21 and a group of 2. The group of 80 percent of Haïti's population receives slightly more than half of the pie, or 51 percent of income. The remaining 10 percent of the population gets what is left: just under 1 percent of the pie. After the class members return to their seats, ask them to share how this exercise made them feel.

Reflect: (15 minutes)

In Chapter 2 (see the section "A Culturally Relevant Theology"), the Rev. Dr. Pierre observes that Haïtian culture is a synthesis of African culture (70 percent), followed by French culture (20 percent) and American and Spanish cultures (10 percent). Ask the class what they think accounts for the differences in cultural influences. To dig a little deeper, follow up with these questions about culture:

- Why is it important for us to be aware of these cultural influences?

- What problems arise when one culture dominates another?

Learn: The Legacy of Colonialism—Debt (15 minutes)

Direct participants' attention to the section "Haïti's Challenges Prior to the Earthquake" in Chapter 5 of the study book. Haïti's debt was part of the legacy of centuries of colonialism. In 2009, thanks in part to the efforts of Jubilee USA Network, Haïti's debt of approximately $1.2 billion was canceled by the World Bank, the International Monetary Fund and the U.S. government, among other lenders. In order to visualize the enormity of that debt, tell the class that if one dollar equaled one foot of string, the string would circle the earth nine times. If you have a globe, wrap a length of string around it nine times.

In order to help class members grasp the disparity in income between Haïti and developed nations, write $3.54 on the chalkboard or newsprint pad and ask participants to call out what they could purchase for that amount. Record their suggestions beneath the number. Next write $55.00 and ask what they could buy with that amount of money. The lists should look significantly different. Reveal that these two amounts represent the median amount of daily income in Haïti ($3.54) versus developing countries ($55.00). These amounts translate to an income of $1,300 per year in Haïti and $20,075 per year in the developed world.

For the next segment ask participants to write down their annual income on a slip of paper and divide it by 365 to get their personal daily income. (You may want to have a calculator on hand.) Assure participants that they will not be asked to publicly share their incomes. Once class members have calculated their daily income, ask them to figure out how many days they need personally to equal an average Haïtian's annual income. Invite class members to write down how they feel about these numbers.

Learn: Folk Wisdom of Haïti (15 minutes)

The Rev. Dr. Pierre has sprinkled proverbs in Creole throughout the study book. Before the session, you will either want to write down each proverb on an individual sheet of paper to pass out to participants or reproduce the sayings (see "Deeper Meaning of the Haïtian Proverbs" for the full list of proverbs) to post around the classroom. Match participants with proverbs (individually, in pairs, or small groups depending on the size of your class) and ask them to write similar or equivalent sayings from American culture. For example, the Creole expression "Lanmò pa gen klaksòn," or "Death does not have a warning bell," is roughly equivalent to the expression "You never know when your number's up" in the United States. Some sayings may give participants trouble. It's all right if there are no equivalent expressions in the United States for the folk sayings of Haïti. Point out to the class that perhaps Haïtians know some things U.S. citizens don't know. It is important to recognize the wisdom of Haïti's people to counterbalance the common misconception that income reflects intelligence. Remind participants that illiteracy—not being able to read or write—indicates a lack of formal education, not necessarily lack of intelligence.

Reflect (5 minutes)

As you prepare to conclude the session, ask participants to think back to the stereotypes of Haïti they had at the beginning of the session and have them reassess their impressions of Haïti now that they have spent some time learning about Haïti's history and culture. After giving them a few moments to reflect silently, ask the class: Have any of your attitudes changed? If so, how? Have participants share their responses in small, informal groups of three or so.

Ask class members to assess their reactions to the oppression and exploitation of the Haïtian people by Spain, France and the United States. Pose these questions for them to silently reflect on: How much did you know previously about this history? How do you reconcile this painful past with the positive cultural influences the Haïtians celebrate today? How can God's message of confession, repentance, forgiveness and reconciliation apply to nations as well as individuals? Ask for a few participants who are willing to share their thoughts with the class.

Closing Worship (5 minutes)

Song: "O Spirit of the Living God," UMH #539

Scripture: Read Acts 2:1-12
Leader: The Word of God for the people of God.
People: Thanks be to God.

Response
Leader: What did it mean that people of every nation heard the good news in their own language at Pentecost? Some people thought it meant the apostles were drunk.
People: No! Not at all! It meant that Christ is Lord of all.
Leader: What does it mean for us today?
People: It means that no single nation can claim exclusive knowledge of the truth of Christ.
Leader: It means that God speaks to people in every nation.
People: It means that God is not confined by our boundaries.

Prayer Song: "This Is My Song," UMH #437

Assignment for Session Two

Read Chapter 2, "Toward a Haïtian Theology of Liberation."

Session 2: The Role of Faith in Social Justice

Introduction

This session will focus on the scriptural underpinnings of social justice and liberation theology in general as well as the Wesleyan tradition of social holiness in particular. For many United Methodists, this discussion is not new. For those who have always belonged to the denomination and grew up with debates in the church over its social principles, this session will be an extension of that conversation. For others, liberation theology will be unfamiliar territory because the focus of many mainstream and nondenominational Christian churches in the United States has been on personal salvation, in which the central faith question to be answered is, "Have you been saved?" Following from that personal focus, mission theology likewise tends to focus its evangelical efforts on the great commission of Matthew 28, "Go, make of all disciples," in which the goal of mission is to win souls for Christ.

Liberation theology challenges Christians to rethink this focus on individual salvation by focusing instead on kingdom theology, which affirms that faith is lived out not alone but within a community. While we ought to cultivate a personal relationship with God, as the first commandment—to love God with all our hearts, minds, soul and strength—affirms, Jesus reminds us that the second commandment is like it—to love our neighbors as ourselves (see Matthew 22:37-39). The letters of John also affirm that it is not possible to love God if we do not love our brothers and sisters. Christians of all persuasions can agree on the centrality of God's love. The point at which many American Christians struggle with liberation theology, however, is its mandate to "act justly." American Christians are accustomed to being generous. They willingly and happily give to charities. They wholeheartedly support food pantries and soup kitchens. But fewer American Christians have devoted as much time, attention and resources to changing social and political systems that keep people trapped in poverty. Because their focus is on personal sin and salvation, they have often been blind to systemic sin in the form of social oppression. Attempts to change social and political systems to redress unjust laws and practices that favor wealthy people and oppress the poor are often labeled "socialism" or "communism." The focus of this session is to provide the biblical foundation for social justice in general and begin to apply liberation theology more specifically to Haïti.

Objectives

In order to provide appropriate assistance to the people of Haïti today, Christians need to understand how colonial powers and the church contributed to the oppression of Haïti's people in the past. Ideally, an understanding of liberation theology will lead to changed practices in the way the church is in mission, namely from "mission to others" to "mission partnership with others."

- To examine what the Bible says about oppression and freedom.

- To learn what the prophets have to say about God's desire for justice.

- To broaden our understanding of the role of faith beyond personal salvation.

What you will need for this session: Bibles, hymnals, paper and pencils.

Opening Worship (10 minutes)

Responsive Reading: Based on Luke 4:18-19
Leader: The Spirit of the Lord is upon me...

People: Holy Spirit, Love Divine, descend on our hearts today,
Leader: because He has anointed me to bring good news to the poor.
People: Inspire us, Prince of Peace, to offer words of hope rather than words of condemnation to the poor.
Leader: He has sent me to proclaim release to the captive and recovery of sight to the blind . . .
People: Give us hearts of compassion, Good Shepherd, to show your love to all people, not just the ones we find acceptable,
Leader: to let the oppressed go free and to proclaim the year of the Lord's favor.
People: That your kingdom may come on earth and your will be done.

Song: "O Young and Fearless Prophet," UMH #444

Prayer

Hear our prayer of confession, Lord of our hearts. Forgive us when we confine you to being a personal friend and savior whose only purpose is to salve our consciences and tell us what good people we are. Forgive us when we forget that you spoke harsh words of judgment to the religious leaders of your day because they were more concerned about their own salvation than about seeking justice for the poor. Help us on this journey of faith to grow beyond the comfort of home and church so that we might be voices proclaiming your truth and working for justice in this world so that your kingdom is no longer simply a pretty dream but evidence of your reign on earth. Amen.

Words of Assurance

Hear these words of assurance: The Lord of our hearts hears and forgives. The God of the prophets calls us to justice and walks with us in new paths of love in action. Amen.

Learn: The Universal and the Contextual in Liberation Theology (10 minutes)

The Rev. Dr. Pierre makes the point that we all interpret the scriptures in light of the place and time in which we live. Our theological task is to sort out those points where faith and culture meet. When is "Christ against culture," as theologian Richard Neibuhr put it, and when is "Christ above culture"? In other words, as we attempt to convey the gospel message, how can we communicate the universal good news of God's love in ways that people in particular times, places and life circumstances will find relevant? The modern origins of liberation theology are rooted in the 1960s and 1970s. Some participants will have lived through those decades and will be able to recall firsthand experiences of those times. Others may have only read about events in history books, and some may be only vaguely aware of what those times were like. Take this first part of the session to provide the backdrop from which liberation theology emerged.

On a whiteboard or newsprint pad, write down these dates at the top: 1960s and 1970s. To one side write "The United States" and ask the class to call out the major historical events of those decades and jot down their responses below. Next write down "Africa" and ask what was happening there during the same decades, again recording their responses. Although you should have no difficulty getting responses to events in the

United States, the group may need encouragement with the historical events in Africa. Come prepared with a couple of suggestions for the list, such as the Mau Mau Uprising in Kenya, the wars of independence in Angola and Namibia among others, Nelson Mandela's imprisonment in 1964 for anti-apartheid activism with the African National Congress (ANC), the Soweto riots in 1976, and Steven Biko's death in 1977. Last, write down "Latin America" on the board and record the class's responses to what was happening there. Again, you may need to have a couple of responses prepared ahead of time, for example Fidel Castro and the revolution overthrowing Batista in Cuba in 1959, the Bay of Pigs in 1961, and Che Guevara and guerilla movements throughout Latin America.

Have the class reflect briefly on the lists of events for each area. What commonalities to do they see among these lists of major events? What is unique in each area? What connections do participants see between the historical events of these decades and the emergence of liberation theology? Have the class review the Haïti timeline (see pp. 7–11) to compare its history with the history of the region.

Liberation Theology—Part 1: Freedom, Not Slavery (20 minutes total)

Sometimes we are so familiar with Bible stories from childhood that we fail to read them later with fresh eyes. The story of Moses confronting Pharaoh and leading the Israelites through the wilderness to the Promised Land is a foundational story of deliverance from slavery.

Read (10 minutes)

Have participants concentrate on Exodus 3:7-10, paying special attention to what God instructs Moses to do from the burning bush. Consider these simple questions (with possible responses) as the class works through the scripture verse by verse:

- What prompts God to rescue the Israelites? *God plans to rescue God's people, the Israelites, from slavery, because God has heard their cries. Slavery is an unacceptable human institution. God stands on the side of freedom.* [handwritten: They cried for freedom]

- Does God place any requirements, preconditions, or administer a litmus test that people must pass in order to be freed from slavery? *No. God is responding to their pleas. There is no "first do this and then I'll set you free." God's will is always for freedom.* [handwritten: do we enslave ourselves?]

- How does God refer to the Israelites? *God calls them "my people." In other words, we belong to God. Also notice that we are God's people, in the plural. God isn't delivering individuals from slavery. God is delivering the whole community of Israelites from slavery.*

- What is God's promise to the Israelites? *The Israelites are not only being delivered from slavery under the Egyptians, but also God promises them a land of their own, flowing with milk and honey. God's plan does not divide the world between the "haves" and the "have-nots." God wants everyone to have what life requires.* [handwritten: They got it via Conquest!]

- What is Moses's role in God's plan? *His role is to speak to Pharaoh and lead the people out of Egypt. When God spoke to Moses, God didn't ask whether Moses had faith in God. God didn't promise to deliver Moses from slavery in Egypt (he was by then a shepherd).*

84 | Study Leader's Guide

Reflect (10 minutes)

After the class has worked through the scripture reading, have them turn in their hymnals to "Go Down, Moses," *UMH* #448. Sing or read verses 1–4 and 11. This African-American spiritual dates from the time of slavery in the United States. The biblical story of the Israelites' slavery in Egypt and their deliverance to the Promised Land spoke to their experience. Ask the class to reflect on how the Exodus story—deliverance from slavery—applies to the story of Haïti's people. Ask these questions:

- Who is Pharaoh? *In the context of Haïti, Pharaoh could be the World Bank, the countries to which Haïti in indebted, or the ruling elite of Haïti.*

- Who are the Israelites? *The Israelites were slaves, and in Haïti, the masses of poor peasants are in the position of slaves. It was Toussaint Louverture, a former slave, who led the slave revolt that won Haïti's independence in 1801, so the Haïtian slaves, like the Israelites, actively sought their freedom.*

- Who is Moses? *God asked Moses to do something on behalf of others, to leave his comfortable life and take on the struggle of his people. In the language of liberation theology, Moses had to surrender his allegiance to Pharaoh, give up his former status of wealth and power and be in solidarity with the people. Those churches and missionaries who seek justice and dignity for the least of Haïti are acting like Moses, leading people to a land of promise.*

A word of caution: Discussion of slavery can be uncomfortable for people for many reasons. For some class members, life experiences may lend to discussing slavery on an intellectual or metaphorical level—"slavery to sin and death" as Saint Paul put it. If some participants have ancestors who were slaves, be sensitive to that situation. While a discussion of being a slave to alcohol or drugs can help some participants identify with the biblical story and while the impact of addictions can be devastating, it is not the same as being the property of another person, to be bought and sold and to be physically and emotionally abused by a master. The scars of slavery can still hurt, so be attentive to the emotional responses of participants.

Break (5 minutes)

Liberation Theology—Part 2: Prophetic Voices for Social Justice (30 minutes)

Following the discussion of God's intervention against slavery, the class will shift to scriptures from the prophets that focus on economic class and oppression. Divide the class half and assign one to focus on Amos 2:6-7 and the other group on Amos 5:21-24 and Micah 6:8. Give the small groups 20 minutes to discuss the questions for reflection, and use the other 10 minutes for the groups to give a summary of their insights to the rest of the class.

Group 1. Read Amos 2:6-7

Reflect: Why should we care how the products we buy are made?

God's judgment against economic oppression is clear. God will not tolerate behavior that denigrates or dehumanizes people. In current language, God's message is "people before profits." Greed is traditionally listed as one of the seven deadly sins. Ask participants to call out current examples of economic injustice in the world, such as child labor, sweatshops, etc. Are they aware of specific economic injustices in regard to Haïti? (If the class isn't aware, you may want to ask a class member to research the history of Haïti's debt, beginning with their independence from France, and report to the class at the next session.)

Ask participants whether they have ever boycotted a product because of unfair labor practices. If anyone has, ask the person to share what product she or he boycotted and why. What was the result of the boycott, if any?

Then ask participants whether they have ever spent more for a product because they were aware of the company's good practices? If participants are unaware of such products, let them know about fair trade coffee and chocolate that they can purchase through UMCOR. Explain how more of the profits from these products end up in the pockets of the people who grow the coffee and cacao rather than big corporations and marketers.

Group 2. Read: Amos 5:21-24 and Micah 6:8

Reflect: What does social justice have to do with worship?

Years ago there was a popular bumper sticker that read: "Honk if you love Jesus." As I sat at a red traffic light behind an SUV, I read this message taped onto its spare tire: "What does the Lord require? Act justly, love mercy and walk humbly with your God. Any old fool can honk." In other words, it's easy to give lip service to belief in God, but as Christians we are expected to put our words of love into concrete action.

1. How much time and effort is spent in your home church on providing a satisfying worship experience? How many people are involved in providing music? How does the verse "Away with the noise of your songs! I will not listen to the music of your harps" make you feel? What do these verses suggest in regard to God's perspective about the purpose of worship? Under what circumstances do you think God is pleased with our worship?

2. How much of your church budget is spent on missions and social justice ministries? What social justice ministries is your church involved with? Does your church have a soup kitchen? Prison ministry? Food pantry? Support a women's shelter? Provide legal aid for immigrants? How many people attend worship compared to the number of people involved in outreach ministries?

3. In what ways is your church engaged in providing justice and social equity for Haïti's people?

Liberation Theology—Part 3: John Wesley and Social Holiness (30 minutes)

Although liberation theology as we speak of it today originated in the tumultuous 1960s and 1970s, the issue of social justice was close to the heart of Methodism's founder, John Wesley. His times were tumultuous as well. Wesley saw the increasing disparity between the wealthy and the poor that resulted from the Industrial Revolution. He not only preached to the poor but also worked tirelessly on their behalf, reforming the worst ills of society. Wesley's inspiration for social holiness was, of course, based on scripture.

Ask the class to read this excerpt from The United Methodist Church website (from the homepage at umc.org, follow the links for "Out Faith," "Beliefs" then "Our Wesleyan Heritage" and scroll down to "Nurture and Mission of the Church"):

For Wesley, there was *no religion but social religion, no holiness but social holiness* [emphasis added]. In other words, faith always includes a social dimension. One cannot be a solitary Christian. As we grow in faith through our participation in the church community, we are also nourished and equipped for mission and service to the world. (*Who Are We? Doctrine, Ministry, and the Mission of The United Methodist Church,* Revised: Leader's Guide by Kenneth L. Carder [Nashville: Cokesbury, 2001], 55.)

Activity: Social Holiness

Make sure that each participant has a *United Methodist Hymnal.* Divide the class into small groups of three or four. Have them turn in their hymnals to the section labeled "Social Holiness." Point out the sections in the index of hymns labeled "Social Concerns" and "Justice" as well. Assign groups to work with specific hymns so they have more time to read and discuss them. Have the groups consider the following questions, reserving some time to have the class as a whole share their observations.

Questions for reflection:

1. What common themes do you notice in this section of hymns?

2. How often does your congregation sing hymns from this section? Frequently? Occasionally? Never? Why do you think that is?

3. How has the prohibition "you should never talk about politics or religion" affected your comfort level in discussing issues of social justice and the church? Has social justice always been a significant part of your faith journey? Or has social justice been irrelevant to your faith journey so far? Why is that?

4. What impact might John Wesley's understanding of social holiness have on how the church engages in mission in Haïti?

Closing Worship (5 minutes)

Song: "We Are Called," TFWS #2172

Affirmation of Faith: "The World Methodist Social Affirmation," UMH #886

Song: "For the Healing of the Nations," UMH #428

Assignment for Session 3

Read the Epilogue, "Hopes and Dreams for Haïti and Its People," and review Chapter 1's material on church history.

Supplement to Talking About Liberation Theology

Some participants may view liberation theology with skepticism or suspicion. If participants challenge the tenets of liberation theology as socialist or communist, take time to address those concerns rather than gloss over them or suppress discussion. Use the resistance as an opportunity for dialogue in which participants define what social justice means to them. Have the class look up Matthew 25:31-46. If providing for those in need is a Christian principle, what does that mean for a country, such as the United States, that claims or aspires to be a "Christian nation"?

Objections to certain phrases such as God's "preferential option for the poor" are fairly common. You may be asked something along the line of, "Isn't that saying God loves poor people more than the wealthy?" Be prepared to respond to such a concern. Reassure participants that they are right that God loves everyone. One way to interpret the phrase "preferential option" is to liken the situation to experiences of parenting. Most participants should have no trouble understanding that they love all of their children (or that their parents loved them along with their siblings), but if one child has a disability, even though you still love all of your children, you may worry more about the child who is most vulnerable. Like any human parent, God has a special concern for those who are most vulnerable: the orphan, the widow and the poor. Invite participants to search a concordance for all the scriptural references to these vulnerable groups in the Bible. Note that God consistently insists that the community provide for the needs of those who are not able to provide for themselves.

Likewise, you may want to point out all of the references in the Bible about the wealthy. What does Jesus have to say about those who are wealthy? Expect some discomfort over passages such as "It is easier for a camel to go through the eye of a needle than for someone who is rich to enter the kingdom of God" (Matthew 19:24; Mark 10:25; Luke 18:25) and "If you wish to be perfect, go, sell your possessions and give the money to the poor, and you will have treasure in heaven. Then come, follow me" (Matthew 19:21; Mark 10:21; Luke 12:33). Are the wealthy automatically condemned? What special responsibilities do the wealthy have? How does our wealth get in the way of our faith? What stereotypes/attitudes do we have toward the poor? Are those the attitudes Jesus held?

Session 3: Preaching a Vision of Hope

Introduction
In Session 2 we looked at the main tenets of a theology of liberation for Haïti. Based on liberation theology's insistence on social justice, we will turn our attention now to the impact this theology has on our concept of mission. To that end, we will look more closely at the history of the church in Haïti, especially examining how it failed in the past to provide a prophetic voice against the inequities of race, class and gender.

The scriptures tell that where there is no vision, the people perish (see Proverbs 29:18, KJV). It is imperative, therefore, for the church to offer a clear vision of hope to the world. We will wrap up the session by developing personal visions of God's kingdom and sharing with one another our visions of hope for Haïti's future.

Objectives
In light of liberation theology, we will examine the changes in the mission field from the colonial era to the current time. The objectives of this session are:

- To confess how the church has been an instrument of oppression in the past.

- To learn how a new model of mission seeks to work in partnership with people, takes a holistic approach in development projects and focuses on communities as much as on individuals.

- To develop personal visions of God's kingdom.

For this session, you will need hymnals, Bibles and art and craft supplies.

Opening Worship (10 minutes)

Song: "Jézu de Nazarèt" ("Jesus of Nazareth")*

  *Available from Global Praise (along with other Haïtian songs) at http://new.gbgm-umc.org/resources/globalpraise/

Scripture: Revelation 21:1-22:6

Prayer
When we see what is wrong in your world, O Creator, give us voices to speak out against injustice and give us hearts of courage to right the wrongs we see. When our strength falters, send your Holy Spirit, so that we can work toward the day when justice prevails and your Holy City arises fair, not in a vision only, but in truth. Amen.

Song: "O Holy City, Seen of John," UMH #726

Learn: The Church's Need to Confess (20 minutes)
What was wrong or misguided about the church's approach to spreading the gospel? Have the class review Chapter 1, especially the section "Religion in Haïti." What was the connection between the conquistadors and the church? What methods did the early Catholic priests use to convert the native peoples of Haïti to Christianity? What was the impact of Protestantism in Haïti?

It can be easy for us to believe that abuses are a thing of the past, so shift the discussion of the church's failings in centuries past to the current state of the church in Haïti. For this segment, have class members turn to the sections "A Brief History of Christianity in Haïti" and "From Elitism to Solidarity with the People" in Chapter 2 to examine the Rev. Dr. Pierre's critique of the church and clergy in Haïti in more recent years. Scholars often critique social systems in regard to race, class and gender inequities, so it can be instructive for Christians to use Paul's proclamation in Galatians 3:28, "There is no longer Jew or Greek, there is no longer slave or free, there is no longer male or female, for all of you are one in Christ Jesus," as our guide for critiquing where the church has hit the mark and where the church still has work to do to bring about oneness in Christ.

Learn and Reflect: Visions for a New Heaven and a New Earth (30 minutes)

In Chapter 5, the Rev. Dr. Pierre wrote: "The hope is that out of the rubble and ashes of the devastation, a new, more developed and prosperous Haïti will rise like a new phoenix. There is indeed hope for better days for Haïti and its people because the potential to rebuild a better and more sustainable country is within reach." That message is echoed in the following videos. View "Haïti: The Politics of Rebuilding" or "Rebuilding Haïti," available for download or desktop viewing (see the Bibliography for Web addresses).

On a chalkboard or newsprint pad, write "City of God" and "Mountain of God." John's vision of the City of God, or the New Jerusalem, which he writes about in Revelation, is based on an image from the Old Testament. Ask class members to turn to Revelation 21:1–22:6 and describe what kind of society John is envisioning, not so much in terms of physical description ("streets paved with gold") but the types of relationships among people and between people and God. Write their responses on the board.

Another common visionary image in the Bible is the "Mountain of God." Have participants turn to Micah 4:1-4 and have someone read it aloud. Have the class reflect on this passage, again focusing on the kind of society Micah envisions. Write the class's responses under "Mountain of God." How is Micah's vision of the Mountain of God similar to John's vision of the New Jerusalem? How do they differ?

Now ask someone to read the vision and hope for Haïti found in the Epilogue. How does the Rev. Dr. Pierre's vision for Haïti compare to the visions of John and Micah?

The rest of the session will now focus on answering this question: What is your vision of God's kingdom?

Break (5 minutes)

Activity: Expressing Our Visions (45 minutes)

Invite participants to express their visions of a "new heaven and a new earth," using whatever creative medium appeals to them. They can write a poem, song or poetic prophecy describing their vision, or they can draw a picture. Have as many different types of media available as you are able to offer: pen and ink, charcoal, pastels, colored pencils, etc. If you have a variety of craft and sewing supplies available, you could invite participants to design and collaborate on making a banner for the sanctuary. Other materials include old magazines that can be cut and pasted into a collage, rubber stamps with inkpads in a variety of colors along with card stock, or modeling clay.

If you have sufficient time and a dedicated group of crafters and artists in your congregation, you might also consider working on a more complex creative project, such as a mosaic made from broken pieces of pottery. If your church has a liturgical dance group, encourage them to choreograph a dance to visually express either Micah 4:1-4 or the visionary scripture found in Isaiah 11:1-9. If your church has a copy of Edward Hicks's painting "The Peaceable Kingdom," put it on display. If not, you can find an image of it on the Internet.

Closing Worship (10 minutes)

Song: "Halle, Halle, Halleluja," TFWS #2026

Responsive Scripture: Isaiah 65:17-25 (NIV)
"New Heavens and a New Earth"

Leader: Behold, I will create new heavens and a new earth. The former things will not be remembered, nor will they come to mind.

People: **But be glad and rejoice forever in what I will create, for I will create Jerusalem to be a delight and its people a joy.**

Leader: I will rejoice over Jerusalem and take delight in my people; the sound of weeping and of crying will be heard in it no more.

People: **Never again will there be in it an infant who lives but a few days, or an old man who does not live out his years.**

Leader: He who dies at a hundred will be thought a mere youth; he who fails to reach a hundred will be considered accursed.

People: **They will build houses and dwell in them; they will plant vineyards and eat their fruit.**

Leader: No longer will they build houses and others live in them, or plant and others eat.

People: **For as the days of a tree, so will be the days of my people; my chosen ones will long enjoy the works of their hands.**

Leader: They will not toil in vain or bear children doomed to misfortune; for they will be a people blessed by the Lord, they and their descendants with them.

People: **Before they call I will answer; while they are still speaking I will hear.**

Leader: The wolf and the lamb will feed together, and the lion will eat straw like the ox.

People: **"They will neither harm nor destroy on all my holy mountain," says the Lord.**

Song: "Be Thou My Vision," UMH #451

Assignment for Session 4

Read Chapter 3, "Gone in 35 Seconds," and Chapter 4, "Links of Solidarity and Partnership."

Session 4: Putting Love in Action

Introduction

Faith is not an end, but a means to an end. Put another way, faith is a first step on the journey, not the destination. Christ invited the first disciples to leave their nets and come follow him. Christ invited the 12 on a journey that would not only transform their lives but also the lives of their neighbors and the people they met along the way. If claiming faith in Christ ends our journey, we have missed the gospel message. Christ modeled for us a life of service to others. We ought to do likewise.

As an educator, I value knowledge and learning. But one of the hard lessons I learned in a graduate course on writing for publication was the professor's insistence that we tackle the big "So what?" question from the outset. Knowledge for its own sake is part of the seduction of academia. Asking "So what?" forces a scholar to step back and get the big picture. Why does this particular information or analysis or case study matter? Why should anyone take the time to read this scholarly paper or book? What will the reader gain?

As a person of faith, I have to ask the same question. Why should I read the Bible? Why should I spend valuable hours of my life learning more about the situation in Haïti? I hope that the answer to the "So what?" question is obvious. The answer is not for personal benefit alone. You attend the School of Christian Mission because you are more than a Christian in name only. You intend to put "Love in Action." The knowledge and insights you gain from reading the Bible and reading mission studies, such as this one, prepare you to better serve your neighbors. To that end, in this session we will focus our attention on the variety of ways in which individuals, groups, churches and other organizations can join in partnership with the people of Haïti in their recovery and rebuilding efforts.

Objectives

- To learn about The United Methodist Church's involvement in Haïti through its denominational structure: The General Board of Global Ministries (GBGM), United Methodist Committee on Relief (UMCOR), United Methodist Volunteers-in-Mission (UMVIM), United Methodist Women and annual conferences.

- To learn how to put love into action on a personal level.

For this session you will need hymnals, construction paper "name" tags, index cards or small slips of paper and pencils and an offering basket.

Worship (10 minutes)

Call to Worship: Based on 2 Samuel 22:7

Leader:	In my distress I called on the Lord;
People:	**to my God I called.**
Leader:	From his temple he heard my voice;
People:	**my cry came to his ears.**

Song: "The Voice of God Is Calling," UMH #451

Prayer

The people of Haïti cried out to you, Lord, and you heard. We, too, have heard their cries. As you did for the Israelites, send an angel to the people of Haïti to guard them along their journey of healing and hope. Grant us the courage and compassion to hear your voice when you call so that we might respond as the people did to Joshua, saying, "Whatever you have commanded us we will do, and wherever you send us we will go" (Joshua 1:16). Amen.

92 | Study Leader's Guide

Song: "The Summons," TFWS #2130

Activity: Links of Solidarity (20 minutes)

This exercise is designed to show the connectional nature of our denomination. Make oversized "name" tags out of 9x12 construction paper, punching holes in the top corners to tie a piece of yarn so the labels can hang around a person's neck. To help participants grasp how the various agencies of the church link together to provide mission support around the world, label the sheets of paper General Board of Global Ministries (GBGM), UMCOR, Mission Volunteers Program, Jurisdictional UMVIM Coordinators, Annual Conference UMVIM Coordinators, United Methodist Women, United Methodist Women Local Unit and L'Église Méthodiste d'Haïti. You can add as many other agencies or organizational levels as you wish: District United Methodist Women, Schools of Mission, other specific program areas of the General Board of Global Ministries, specific mission projects and/or missionaries or a generic "mission trip." You may also want several sheets of paper labeled "Me." Ideally, everyone in the class should have a label for this exercise.

Distribute the labels, and then ask the person who has the General Board of Global Ministries label to stand in the center of an open area of the classroom where there will be sufficient space for class members to link themselves together. Ask the class what agencies make up the General Board of Global Ministries— UMCOR and United Methodist Women, for example. Ask them to link arms or join hands with the GBGM person. Guide the class through the various links and show how they relate to one another. The class will form lines sprawling out from the GBGM. One chain, for example, would start with GBGM, then the Mission Volunteers Program, linking to the Jurisdictional UMVIM coordinators, to annual conference UMVIM coordinators, to mission trips, and end with "me." Another chain would start with GBGM, then United Methodist Women, Conference United Methodist Women, District United Methodist Women and finally United Methodist Women Local Unit and "Me." Some of the lines will interconnect, similar to a spider's web.

Reflect

When participants have returned to their seats, have them reflect on the organizational structure of the church. In what ways is the structure hierarchical? In what ways is it horizontal in structure? How is this structure helpful? (And perhaps, where is it confusing?) Most important, how could/should/does the structure facilitate a partnership model of mission with the people of Haïti?

Learn: Closer Look at the Links (30 minutes)

Now that the class has gotten an overview of how the various mission outreach programs of the church fit together, divide the class into three groups so participants can get a closer look at some of the programs, specifically UMCOR, UMVIM and covenant relationships. Give the groups 20 minutes to read and discuss their material, and provide 10 minutes for the groups to report to the rest of the class (roughly 3 minutes each).

Group 1: What is UMCOR doing in Haïti?

If you have access to the Internet in your classroom, check to see if you can set up a computer so the group can navigate the UMCOR website. Don't assume that everyone is familiar with all of the work UMCOR does. If the group can't access the Internet, direct the group's attention to the information in Chapter 4 on UMCOR as well as information in Appendix B, and make available issues of **response**, *New World Outlook* and

Interpreter that include articles on Haïti. Have the group scan through the articles, identify the supported mission projects and institutions and report to the rest of the class.

Group 2: What is UMVIM doing?

United Methodist Volunteers-in-Mission coordinate mission trips throughout the United States and the world by working in conjunction with UMVIM coordinators in the five jurisdictions and annual conferences of The United Methodist Church in the United States. A special UMVIM pilot project has been set up to coordinate projects in Haïti. If you have Internet access in your classroom, have this group access the website at umvimHaiti.org. A portion of the material can be found in Appendix B, "Haïti Response Project Overview." The group should read through the document and report to the class on the components of the project that are culturally sensitive. In other words, have the group find examples of how this document teaches what is considered proper by Haïtian standards that are different from American culture.

Group 3: Covenant relationships—What are annual conferences doing?

Suggest that the group review some covenants in the Bible: Genesis 9:8-17; 17:1-10; and Jeremiah 31:31-33. Then have the group read the covenant statements from the Michigan Area (West Michigan and Detroit Conferences; see Appendix D) and the Florida Conference (see Appendix E). Ask them to identify the nature of the relationships that these conferences have formally established and how they reflect the concepts of solidarity or partnership.

Break: 5 minutes

Learn: Mission Project Case Study: HAPI (30 minutes)

Give the class time to review the material in Appendix C about Haïtian Artisans for Peace International (HAPI). Again, if you have Internet access, some class members may want to access the HAPI website for more detailed information. One of the ideals that the founders and the board of directors of HAPI have striven to implement in how HAPI operates is that the organization should embody a holistic approach in providing assistance. Ask the class to look for evidence of a holistic approach to mission.

Reflect

One way in which the class can evaluate HAPI's holistic approach is to look for evidence of how the project addresses the needs of whole persons—their bodies, minds and souls. Write those words on the board and have the participants call out examples for each category.

Another way of understanding a holistic approach is to look for evidence that the project serves as leaven for the whole community in addition to helping individuals. On the board write "individual" and "community." Have the class call out examples of how HAPI improves the lives of the individual women who are part of the collective and then how the project helps the community of Mizak beyond the women directly involved in HAPI.

Putting Love Into Action (15 minutes)

We all have many causes we want to support, but we also know that our finances and time have limits, and so at some point we have to target our efforts to one or two causes to which we will devote our greatest attention. On the other hand, Jesus demonstrated that miracles can happen despite how large the problem appears when we use the resources available to us. Ask someone to read the story of the feeding of the five thousand found in Luke 9:10-17.

Suggest to the class that they may want to close their eyes as you walk them through this exercise of imagining themselves taking part in the story from Luke. Ask the class first to put themselves in the place of the five thousand. In a calming voice, say something like,

- You are far from your village and home.

- You are hungry, but you came to hear Jesus preach and to be healed.

- You overhear what the disciples say to Jesus: "Send them away."

- How do you feel?

- How are the people of Haïti like the five thousand?

Pause between statements so that participants have time to visualize the scene. Then have the class open their eyes. Ask for a couple of participants to share responses.

Now ask the class to put themselves in the place of the disciples. Using the same technique, say,

- You see the huge crowd and your stomach is rumbling with hunger.

- You know that this crowd is mostly people of meager means who probably didn't have much to eat before they came out to meet Jesus.

- You are sure that they are getting hungry, too. The sensible thing to do is tell Jesus to send them away.

- When you do, he tells you, "You feed them." How do you feel?

When they open their eyes, ask a couple of people to share their feelings.

Take some time now to reflect individually on what your resources are—what are your five loaves and two fish? What can you contribute to feed the five thousand? What can you do to help the people of Haïti? Have class members jot down their ideas. They will be asked to commit to acting on one of their ideas during the commitment time in the closing worship service.

Closing Worship (15 minutes)

Song: "Faith, While Trees Are Still in Blossom," UMH #508

Scripture: Isaiah 9:4; Matthew 11:29-30 (NIV)
Hear these words from the Old Testament:

> For as in the day of Midian's defeat,
>   you have shattered
> the yoke that burdens them,
>   the bar across their shoulders,
>   the rod of their oppressor.

Listen now to these words of Christ:

Haïti: Challenges and Hope | 95

Take my yoke upon you and learn from me, for I am gentle and humble in heart, and you will find rest for your souls. For my yoke is easy and my burden is light.

Litany

Leader: *Se nan malè ou konnen ki moun ki zanmi w.* [Say nahn mahl oo koh-naw key moon key zawn-mee-oo.]

People: **It is in trouble you know who is your friend.**

Leader: The people of Haïti have seen much adversity.

People: **The people of Haïti are looking to us for true friendship.**

Leader: *Men anpil chay pa lou.* [Mawn on-peel shay pah loo.]

People: **Many hands make the load lighter.**

Leader: The task of recovery in Haïti is enormous.

People: **Together, our hands can accomplish miracles.**

Leader: The work has begun.

People: **We will not quit until the work is done.**

Act of Commitment

Give participants an index card and ask them to write down one action they plan to take to assist the people of Haïti. When everyone has written down their act of love on behalf of Haïti, participants should place their commitment cards in an offering plate or basket. Then offer the following prayer as a consecration of the gifts of service.

Closing Prayer

We thank you, God, for all the blessings you have given us. You challenge us to follow your way, and so we ask you to open our minds to hear your word and give us hearts of love that we might share what we have with those who have little. Open our eyes, Lord, to see opportunities to be in mission with the world, and open our souls to the promptings of your Spirit. All this we pray in the name of the One who came to be servant of all, Jesus the Christ. Amen.

Song of Dedication: "Here I Am, Lord," UMH #593

Addendum: Haïtian Artisans for Peace International: A Case Study

Arts are sometimes viewed as a luxury, but in Mizak, a town of 35,000 near Jacmel, Haïti, the arts are a source of income that also provides women with a sense of community. HAPI, Haïtian Artisans for Peace International, exemplifies a new way of "doing" mission. According to Valerie Mossman-Celestin, co-founder of HAPI and a member of West Michigan Conference, HAPI aspires to generate sustainable development and to provide holistic assistance to the community.

HAPI's initial focus was to create income for women by marketing their hand-embroidered cards to churches in the United States. Their creative product line has since expanded to include journals, quilt kits, soap and bags and wallets. But that's not all. The women have begun to tackle other community issues. HAPI has generated several interrelated projects. HAPI offers a variety of classes to the community of Mizak; among them are classes in art, English and theology. Art classes are a natural extension of HAPI's economic focus, but so are English classes because English is a primary language for international business.

HAPI hired its own health care worker to serve the Mizak community. What pleases Mossman-Celestin is how the women are assessing their needs and determining for themselves what to do. For too long, mission was paternalistic in approach. Missionaries came into a community, identified needs and organized projects to meet those needs. While schools and hospitals were built to serve the community, an unintended outcome was to foster the community's dependence on the missionaries and the church's charity. The goal of missions in the 21st century is to foster self-sufficiency instead. HAPI is well on the way to breaking the pattern of learned helplessness among the women.

HAPI is now also a "Communities of Shalom" (COS) site. Begun in the aftermath of the Los Angeles riots in 1992, COS is now international in scope. You can find out more about Communities of Shalom at their website (www.communitiesofshalom.org). Especially helpful to understanding a holistic approach to mission is the section on COS's core values, which include spiritual growth, multicultural harmony, economic prosperity and health, healing and wholeness.

Read more about HAPI in Appendix C or on their website: http://www.unitedmethodistwomen.org/news/articles/item/index.cfm?id=241&pv=1.

Appendixes

Appendix A
The Clinton Foundation Press Release

PRESIDENT CLINTON BREAKS GROUND ON EMERGENCY SHELTER IN HAÏTI
AUGUST 06, 2010 | NEW YORK, NY | CLINTON FOUNDATION | PRESS RELEASES

Shelter is first among dozens to be created following the Clinton Foundation's $1 million commitment to hurricane safety

New York — Today, President Clinton initiated construction on the first project generated by the Interim Haïti Reconstruction Commission (IHRC), by breaking ground on a new communal hurricane shelter at The École Communautaire Sainte Thérèse de Darbonne, a school in Léogâne, Haïti. In June, at the request of Léogâne residents, President Clinton announced a $1 million commitment by the Clinton Foundation to establish and improve communal shelters in areas at risk of hurricane damage. The project was approved by the Board of the IHRC at its first meeting on June 17.

Today, President Clinton also announced that, inspired by the Clinton Foundation's commitment, the American Red Cross is investing $1 million to develop additional emergency shelters and will invest $4 million more as other shelter sites are identified. The Inter-American Development Bank and the World Bank also have committed to invest $1 million and $2 million, respectively, to emergency shelters in Haïti.

Together, this should enable the development of dozens of shelters. Importantly, the structures are designed to serve as schools when there is no storm risk. The Clinton Foundation is contracting with a Haïtian firm and international firm to develop the structures. Approximately 1 to 2 million people in Haïti are still living in temporary settlements and camps throughout the country following the January 12 earthquake. Léogâne is at high-risk for hurricane damage, and currently has 200,000 people living in camps.

Since the earthquake, the Clinton Foundation has facilitated the donation of $25 million to relief efforts and other areas. This includes the disbursement of funds to organizations working on the ground in Haïti as well as the shipment and delivery of emergency, relief, education and agricultural supplies worth over $16 million.

While in Haïti, President Clinton also met with Haïtian Prime Minister Jean-Max Bellerive and President René Préval and participated in meetings with Haïtian ministers and leaders in the private sector.

Appendix B
Haïti Response Project Overview

Excerpt from UMVIM Haïti website
http://new.gbgm-umc.org/about/us/mv/Haiti/plan/
April 2010

The Coordination Team

The Rev. Gesner Paul, President of the EMH (Église Méthodiste d'Haïti), our primary host in Haïti

Susan J. Meister, U.S.–Haïti Calendaring Consultant, Haitivolunteers@yahoo.com

The Rev. Mike Willis, Volunteer Management Coordinator

Douglas Nagle, Finance and Hospitality Coordinator

Donette Lataillade, Manager of the Methodist Guest House in Port-au-Prince, vimhaiti@hotmail.com

Belorne Emile, Assistant Coordinator, second in charge of the Methodist Guest House, belornelazr@yahoo.fr

GBGM Mission Volunteers Office and the five Jurisdictional Coordinators have oversight of the entire process.

Find your Jurisdictional Coordinator contact information at:

http://new.gbgm-umc.org/about/us/mv/mission-teams-umvim/jurisdl-umvimcoords/

Address to Use on Visitor Cards

> Methodist Guest House
> 105 Delmas
> Impasses A Thoby #3
> Petionville, Haïti

All teams will fly into and out of the airport in Port-au-Prince. All team members must arrive and depart at the same time. Team members will likely stay overnight at the Methodist Guest House and be transported to another work site on day two. The team members will also stay overnight at the Guest House the evening before their departure. (In some cases, if the work site is nearby to the MGH, the teams will be at that location for the entire stay.)

Worksite Information

Over the next three years (April 2010–April 2013), teams will be needed to complete the priority projects of the Eglise Methodiste d'Haïti. This is a long-term proposal being worked on with the Rev. Gesner Paul and the Jurisdictional UMVIM Coordinators. Since the Rev. Gesner Paul asked us to stay at or near the projects as a community and relationship building gesture, we will do our best to honor that request. Which means some teams will be in temporary shelters, others in Methodist Guest House situations. Each team will be apprised where they are going a few weeks ahead of when they arrive.

A frequently asked question: Will we be able to work in the area and project site that we have been going to for years? The answer: Not necessarily! We will work on the project list of The Methodist Church of Haïti, having several projects going at once, but carefully and methodically finishing projects before moving on to the next. If you decide to go to Haïti and work as a UMVIM team outside the newly formed Haïti Response Project, thank you! We would like to know that we can track your mission service; please e-mail your schedule to haitivolunteers@yahoo.com. Please note that if you work on a non-priority project, you will not be scheduled through the U.S.–Haïti Calendaring Consultant and your team will not be eligible for matching grants. We ask that teams respect the decisions of the EMH and Haïti consultants, which are based on what is best for the connectional family of United Methodist churches in Haïti rather than on what is best for a particular church or UMVIM team.

Once a team is scheduled and assigned a work site, the team leader will be in contact with the Haïti staff to finalize budgets, transportation, lodging, interpreters, security and cooks. These arrangements may vary slightly site to site. In addition, the Haïti staff will advise the teams on which tools, if any, to bring. The Haïti staff is responsible for arranging for materials and Haïtian workers at the sites. If there is no or sporadic electricity at a site, the Haïti staff will work to help the team have access to a generator.

How Are Project Funds Handled?

1. Teams will submit project funds to the U.S.–Haïti Calendaring Consultant at least six weeks in advance of their departure date.

2. The U.S.–Haïti Calendaring Consultant will forward the funds to GBGM Mission Volunteers and request matching funds.

3. Team project funds along with a matching amount (if qualified from UMCOR grant) to an account setup in Haïti accessed by the Haïti Project or Financial/Host Consultants.

4. Funds will be utilized for materials, the hiring of Haïtian workers/foreperson, and a 5 percent project management fee to the EMH—as per agreement with the Rev. Gesner Paul. Project management to the EMH is an administrative fee for work performed to upkeep all administrative needs of the project (e.g., vouchers, bookkeeping, office supplies). This had been standard operating practice for most EMH/UMVIM sites prior to the earthquake with adjustments by location.

5. Funds will be accounted for and administered by the Haïti Financial/Host Consultant.

It is a part of the Haïtian culture that they expect there to be a "Boss" of any project. In most day-to-day matters this will be the team leader. However, the "financial boss" will be the Haïti Financial/Host Consultant. It is important for Haïtian workers to know that the Haïti Financial/Host Consultant will be paying most of the bills. The Haïti Project Consultant, in consultation with the local church pastor and the Circuit Superintendent, will make sure there is a project director and Haïtian work crew, security for housing (if necessary), cooks and water.

The in-country costs (food, lodging and purchased water) are approximately $40/person/day and can be paid directly to the Haïti Finance Coordinator when you arrive in Haïti. The Haïti Financial/Host Consultant will pay for the food, cook, lodging, security (if needed) and water from these funds.

The team leader will be responsible for transportation costs (gas is usually included in the price of the vehicle), drivers, translators, clothes washing and any special tips that surface during the trip. Please know that tips are a standard staple in the culture of Haïti. Once a team has been scheduled by the U.S.–Haïti Calendaring Consultant, the team leader will finalize budgets and other items with the Haïti Project and Financial/Host Consultants in Haïti.

Suggested Packing List

___ Bible

___ Devotional materials

___ Journal and pen

___ Flashlight

___ A couple of SteriPens™ (a portable water purification device) and team with extra batteries—just in case

___ First aid kit for the work site, not with the medical team component

___ Tools to use and leave to replenish the tool shed at the Methodist Guest House or other locations—this is the Rev. Paul's suggestion; check with the Haïti office for current needs

___ Old work clothing (long pants)—shorts are not culturally acceptable in Haïti for men or women—and they are also not safe on a worksite from injury or sunburn (skirts are okay for appropriate tasks)

___ Sleeping bag or pad with twin sheets

___ Sleeved shirts/blouses (no tank tops, no guys taking shirts off)

___ Water bottle

___ Cotton work gloves

___ Changes of clothing for after work

___ Disposable face masks if doing deconstruction work

___ Personal hygiene items

___ Two towels and two washcloths

___ Work shoes/boots/heavier tennis shoes—no sandals/open-toed shoes on the work site

___ Insect repellent

___ Gel hand sanitizer

___ Sunscreen

___ Dress clothes for church

___ Toilet paper

___ Light colored hat with a brim for sun protection

___ Sunglasses/separate set of prescription glasses

___ Mosquito netting/earplugs—check with the Haïti office

___ Your own stash of Cipro, Pepto or Immodium

___ Double set of any meds you need

Appendix C
Haïtian Artisans for Peace International (HAPI)

THE FOLLOWING INFORMATION IS EXCERPTED FROM THE HAPI WEBSITE: WWW.HAITIANARTISANS.COM.

Mizak Profile

Mizak is a mountainous, rural section of La Vallee in southeast Haïti, 80 km south of Port-au-Prince and 12 km west of Jacmel. The total population is just over 35,000. Seventy percent are peasants living under the poverty level of less than $1-U.S. per day, and 63 percent of the population is under the age of 18. There are no jobs available, no electricity, no telecommunication system, no plumbing and no water filtration. The majority of households have no measurable income and they rely on system of barter and trade.

Agriculture

Agriculture is the main—and unreliable—source of livelihood. Primary agricultural products include corn, a variety of beans and pitimi (similar to millet), as well as many tropical fruits, including oranges, grapefruit, papaya, mangoes and bananas. A typical meal consists of corn or millet meal with bean sauce. A wide variety of livestock is found in Mizak, although meat is seldom included in the diet. Cattle, pigs, goats, chickens, guinea hens and rabbits as well as pack animals such as donkeys, mules and horses can be seen tied to trees or near the homes of people in Mizak.

Women travel long distances to market agricultural goods and may fall victim to rape or theft in the marketplace or become the victim of unsafe transportation. Roads are very poor in Mizak and travel is dangerous. They lose profit in transportation costs and also lose family time. Families are extremely vulnerable to any emergency situation or a bad crop. Adolescents and

A man hoes his field of corn in the Haïtian village of Mizak. *(Paul Jeffrey)*

Children gather for an educational activity sponsored by the local Methodist church in the Haïtian village of Mizak.
(Paul Jeffrey)

young adults often emigrate to Port-au-Prince or the Dominican Republic. They often fall into delinquency or prostitution because of lack of marketable skills and massive unemployment rates. Some return pregnant or ill for the community to care for.

Education
There is a public national school, primary and secondary Catholic schools and many private primary schools spread throughout the 24 zones. However, most schools in Haïti charge tuition, so educational opportunities are usually limited to one child in the family or many times sacrificing family food for education. There are no opportunities for adult education or training. Those with higher education often leave the area, resulting in a "brain drain."

Religious Life
Faith is important in Haïti, and there are two Catholic churches and many Protestant churches. Many people participate in some type of religious community.

The nearest large city is Jacmel, which is about an hour drive, or a four-hour walk, at the bottom of the mountain. Jacmel is considered a cultural and artistic center in Haïti known for its history of architecture, painting, music and its renowned Carnival celebration, as well as its beautiful beaches.

Community Goodwill
In a culture where almost half of the people are illiterate and most never finish secondary school, people in Mizak thirst for opportunities to learn. In addition to the economic opportunities afforded by HAPI, artisans and community members look to HAPI to provide other ways to improve their situation. This enthusiasm resulted in the creation of several classes now offered through the co-op—English, theology and art.

The Arts
HAPI art classes focus on seeing more in their surroundings and bringing this into their paintings. The work created by students has been featured in galler-

A man in Mizak, Haïti, works with his neighbors to create handicrafts that their organization, Haïtian Artisans for Peace International, sells internationally to generate income in the poor rural community. *(Paul Jeffrey)*

ies in the United States and has become popular with HAPI customers. Several paintings have been used on our special Painted Card Sets. The painters have also been using their skills to beautify their community with murals.

English
Students in the English class gain confidence with the language, hoping that their abilities will contribute to the success and independence of HAPI as a business in the international market. Learners gather up to three times a week and are led by local advanced students and supplemented by U.S. volunteers. These classes are open to the community and many varied ages welcomed the opportunity to learn more.

Theology
Faith is an important part of Haïtian life, and more formal study is well received. Several young adults have been inspired to become leaders in a new church formed in Mizak.

New Church Start
The young congregation is an outcome of HAPI, not a program that was initiated by HAPI. Community members and HAPI leadership are not required to attend this church in order to participate in any of HAPI's programs.

Local leadership requested educational resources in Methodist theology, polity and social principles. From this beginning, a pastoral staff of 15 people rooted in Wesleyan principles emerged under the leadership of senior lay preacher and HAPI's director, Paul Prevost. Adult education and services are held on Sunday mornings in the co-op facility.

The church is currently independent of denominational affiliation and does not receive monetary funding from HAPI. Efforts are underway to ratify the church with The Methodist Church of Haïti. Future plans supported by HAPI include additional development of pastoral staff and lay speakers. HAPI may enlist teams for building, vacation Bible school or other events. The church will develop its own community outreach independent of HAPI programs, but HAPI will help to manage the fund development and building of a facility in the future.

Music
UJECE, which is the abbreviation for Union des Jeunes Chanteurs de L'Evangile (Group of Young Gospel Singers), is the singing group that began as part of the worship gatherings. Creating a CD of their songs and doing performances in other communities. Their harmonizing is a wonderful way of sharing their talents.

Healthy Living
Mizak Clinic—In July 2009, a clinic was opened in a separate rented facility for our community health initiatives. Yollande Zephir is a full-time health worker at the facility, which is opened a minimum of 30 hours per week. She will help to administer the Medika Mamba program and do blood pressure screenings and limited diagnostics. HAPI will also offer health seminars, pilot a co-fortified salt program in relationship with the University of Notre Dame and host medical teams in this facility. Research is being done on maternal delivery practices and causes of the high mortality rate that we can use for future healthy mom and baby care.

Medika Mamba—Nutritional intervention with Ready-to-Use Therapeutic Food to severely malnourished children under the age of five helps to ensure that children remain well-nourished and healthy through the toddler years, giving them a chance for normal growth and development into adulthood.

Medika Mamba is an energy dense peanut butter, significantly fortified with protein and nutritional supplements. The name *Medika Mamba* means "peanut butter medicine" in the Haïtian Creole language. It is manufactured in Haïti.

HAPI utilizes community health workers trained in the protocol to dispense the mamba in the home, training the families in proper dosage, chlorinated water treatment and basic hygiene measures to reduce/eliminate diarrheal diseases in the child that deplete their bodies of nutrition. Families come to the clinic once weekly for weigh-ins and documentation of progress.

This was a 2008 pilot, under the direction of a U.S. volunteer. Beginning in July 2009, HAPI hired full-time health worker, Yollande Zephir, to oversee the program. HAPI has a separate clinic facility and we will have three-month rotations of approximately 15 children per rotation on the protocol. Part-time health workers will be hired on an as-needed basis for the mamba administration.

This initiative supports HAPI's mission for healthy communities, job creation for poverty reduction and gender equality with the cultivation of primarily women health workers.

Health Seminars—In the spring of 2009, HAPI offered instruction on a variety of hygiene and health topics for the community. The seminar was entirely Haïtian, led by a Haïtian-American pre-med student and local leadership. Specific training was offered to 12 community health workers on patient intake and taking vital measurements, such as blood pressure. Health training has included a seminar on co-fortified salt to introduce iodine into the local diet and prevent lymphatic filiarisis, as well as training in hygiene, hand washing and clean water. HAPI has also hosted seminars in dental care and women's issues, including "family planning beads. We plan to expand the topics offered and the frequency of seminars in the future and incorporate lessons into the Peace Pals program.

Age Level Programs

Peace Pals

HAPI is a presence for peace in the world, starting with their children. HAPI "Peace Pals" are young people ages 5–15 who are learning to become peacemakers dedicated to living in the spirit of the words May Peace Prevail on Earth.

The Peace Pals Program fosters understanding and respect for the diversity and oneness of the human family and the natural world through the arts, education, communication and friendship and to put those thoughts into action by doing simple and small acts of kindness. Providing a safe and healthy environment for the children to play and learn lessons that HAPI hopes will lead to generational changes in attitude towards self-worth, care for the environment, personal health and hygiene, healthier conflict resolution and respect for all persons.

Peace Pals started meeting once per month in August 2007 with 30 children and now has up to 250 children at their weekly Saturday meetings. They have simple lessons related to peace led by community volunteers, mostly young adults under the supervision of HAPI's Coordinator of Age-Level Ministries, Dominique Verenite. The Peace Pal kids also do special events at the new church congregation, such as a Mother's Day program or performing songs at the Peace Pole dedication.

Originally, it was suggested the Peace Pals be split into two groups—ages 5–10 and 10–15 years—thinking that each group would require different levels of activity. The Haïtians explained that they keep them in one group because it may be that the 15-year-old never experienced a crayon before or never heard a simple lesson on how to live peacefully with your neighbor. It's difficult to imagine that a child in kindergarten here may have experienced more than a 15-year-old in Haïti!

Future goals:

- Hot lunch component.
- Plant trees in the Peace Park.
- Recognize each child's birthday.
- Have a larger Christmas celebration.

In addition, there is a second community that is eager for a Peace Pals program.

Peace Pole

To show Mizak's commitment to peace, a Peace Pole was erected on September 21, 2008, on donated land that will eventually become a park for children. The Peace Pole was a gift of the Grand Rapids District Peace with Justice Community to HAPI. To read about the peace pole dedication and day-long celebration, see our newsletter, issue 2. To learn more about the Peace Pole Project, including information on how to obtain your own Peace Pole, visit http://www.worldpeace.org/activities_peacepoleproject.html.

Peace Park

There are kids everywhere in Mizak, but safe places to play are scarce. The vision of HAPI is to create an ambitious new Peace Park on the donated land. Construction has already begun, transforming an empty field into the beginnings of a community playground.

A "Peace Park" under construction in the Haïtian village of Mizak. *(Paul Jeffrey)*

Phase 1: Clear the land and erect a fence and gate.

Mizak is a rural community and many people use a toxic plant as a barrier to keep animals from entering their property. The plant is highly acidic and the sap burns the skin and can cause blindness if it gets in the eyes. Some communities do not permit it because of the danger, particularly to children. While the park does need some type of barrier to protect against the possibility of any stray animals entering the playground area, the traditional, high concrete wall doesn't send the desired message of openness and invitation. It is also important to easily keep the children in view. It was decided to make an ambitious plan and design a fence with iron fence posts and a traditional gate.

Phase 2: Equipment

Plans have been drawn out that show some swings and playground equipment. Most important, a community overhead shelter with tables and lighting where the youth can gather to study and be in community.

Phase 3: Latrine area

The final phase is to construct a latrine area and hopefully onsite water access. Peace Pals and community volunteers will do the landscaping.

HAPI is registered as an Advance Special #3020490.

108 | Appendixes

Appendix D
Haïti–Michigan Covenant

"Partnership in Mission"

Haïti District of the Methodist Church in the Caribbean and the Americas

Michigan Area of The United Methodist Church
(Albion College, Albion, Michigan)
(Adrian College, Adrian, Michigan)

In thankful recognition and faithful allegiance to the Holy Spirit's call, that equips and enables the Church Community to be in ministry and mission, we join in partnership for Christ, and we respond in faith and love by reaching beyond boundaries in mutual servanthood. The Haïti District of the Methodist Church in the Caribbean and the Americas and the Michigan Area of The United Methodist Church join together their gifts and graces in a shared vision of ministry.

Together we share in the general concept of ministry expressed by a community of faith responding to Christ's mandate of word and deed,

> The Spirit of the Lord is upon me, because he has anointed me to preach good news to the poor. He has sent me to proclaim release to the captives and recovering of sight to the blind, to set at liberty those who are oppressed, to proclaim the acceptable year of the Lord. (Lespri bondie-a sou mouin. Li chouazi-m pou-m anonse bon nouvel la bav pov vo. Li vove-m pou-m fe tout prizonie you konnin vo lage, pou-m fe tout aveg yo konnin yo kabab oue anko, pou-m delivre moun vao maltrete vo, pou-m fe konnin le-a rive pou Bondie vi-n delivre pep li-a.). (Luke 4:18-19)

Our purpose and objective for formalizing our covenant in mission acknowledges our history together in following the biblical imperative to proclaim, preach, release, recover and serve as Christ's people in a waiting and wanting world. Our evoked relationship is also expressed in our Wesleyan tradition that proclaims that the world is our parish. This relationship has been experienced through many years of bonded commitment that has established lasting friendships and the exchange of a cooperative spirit of servanthood.

We enter into this partnership relationship recognizing that neither the Haïti District nor the Michigan Area exists as an autonomous entity but that the Haïti District is one of the eight districts that comprise the Conference of the Methodist Church in the Caribbean and the Americas and, likewise, the Michigan Area is but one of the several areas that constitute The United Methodist Church. We shall conduct this partner relationship with each partner respecting this same basic relationship that exists on the one hand between the Haïti District and the Methodist Church in the Caribbean and the Americas and, on the other hand, the Michigan Area and The United Methodist Church as well as the existing concordat between the Methodist church in the Caribbean and the Americas and The United Methodist Church.

We also acknowledge the years of cooperation expressed by UMCOR in the compassionate ministry to help people to help themselves. We celebrate a long history of working and sharing Christ's vision for his church.

In this symbolic compact of cooperation and respect, we affirm our statement of purpose:

1. The general terms of this cooperative vision between the Haïti District of the Methodist Church in the Caribbean and the Americas and the Michigan Area of the United Methodist Church will be in accord with the covenant already in place between the MCCA (Methodist Church in the Caribbean and the Americas) and the UMC (United Methodist Church).

2. The cooperative projects and programs in which we enter will be those initiated by the Haïti District of the Methodist Church in the Caribbean and the Americas and in accord with the General Board of Global Ministries and UMCOR. The Michigan Area will not enter in or initiate in Haïti any projects and/or programs without the full approval of the leadership of the Haïti District of the Methodist Church in the Caribbean and the Americas.

3. The sending of Volunteer in Mission persons from the Michigan Area will be to cooperate in projects in agreement with the Haïti District of the Methodist Church in the Caribbean and the Americas. No volunteer should displace a worker in Haïti; every effort should be made to hire and employ local workers. It is further required that work teams from both autonomous churches work together on projects.

4. A. The financial arrangements could be channeled through the General Board of Global Ministries or approved Advance Specials. B. Churches and UMVIM Teams are requested to remit all funds for Haïti through the treasurers' offices of the Detroit or West Michigan Annual Conferences (and include reporting procedures on activities and finances). Funds or commitments of support should not be given without the approval of the chairperson of the Haïti District of the Methodist Church in the Caribbean and the Americas.

5. There shall be both an exchange of information and an established process to evaluate the various projects and their socio-economic and spiritual impact. It is hoped that a representative group from each church body will review the progress of this partnership commitment with regular visitation teams.

6. There shall be an exchange of leadership between the Michigan Area and the Eglise Methodiste d'Haïti. Encounter and work teams shall itinerate throughout both connections to interpret the work and to cultivate support.

7. All persons visiting Haïti or Michigan shall have an orientation program in order to be familiar with the culture and the moral standards of the host church.

8. The Michigan Area Task Force on Haïti and the Haïti District of the Methodist church in the Caribbean and the Americas will work together in preparation of a "Needs List" for supplies and materials to be sent to Haïti. This "Needs List" will be made available to all congregations in the Michigan Area.

9. The Michigan Area will actively encourage missionary support through the General Board of Global Ministries for those serving in Haïti to assist the Haïtian church to employ national church workers. (Global Partners in Mission)

10. We will encourage all our congregations to offer prayers of intercession on the first Sunday of each month. We will be in prayer for one another, our shared programs and for those who labor together for Christ in our own places of calling.

11. All those traveling to Haïti and Michigan are required to be in accordance with the policies of the Michigan Area and the Haïti District of the Methodist Church in the Caribbean and the Americas for foreign and domestic sponsored mission encounter teams. This policy will require proper identification, insurance coverage, health coverage and proper orientation and preparation for a cultural encounter. It is suggested that an opportunity for debriefing be provided for those returning from the mission experience.

12. It is agreed that all UMC ministers who are to be sent out to serve in the Haïti District under the auspices of the Covenant shall do so only under the General Board of Global Ministries through which agency the negotiations with the Haïti conference of the Methodist Church in the Caribbean and the Americas shall be conducted. No minister shall serve or function as a resident minister whose status has not been cleared by the Methodist Church in the Caribbean and the Americas.

13. It is understood that one of the main objectives of this covenant is the development of mutual understanding, friendship and solidarity between the two communities by building bridges in the sharing of gifts and graces as well as experiences, concerns and hopes.

Lastly, we look forward to this covenant relationship that will help us mutually to broaden our vision and make us more sensitive to the evils of hunger, injustice, persecution and exploitation at the local and global levels and to the necessity of building a more just and sustainable world. The Haïtian Church continues to be a vital witness of what God's people can do when they hold high the vision of hope. Their vision of hope has enabled them to build an impressive network of churches, schools, health care facilities and dedicated leadership to communicate that hope. The vision of hope has remained strong and vital even when oppressed and dominated by political and economic structures. The Michigan Area and the Haïti District of the Methodist Church in the Caribbean and the Americas join hands to fight against evil and injustice in their own communities.

We give thanks to almighty God for this shared spiritual journey.

Signed by the Reverend Moise L. D. Isidore, General Superintendent and Chairperson, Haïti District of the Methodist Church in the Caribbean and the Americas; Bishop Donald Ott, Resident Bishop of the Michigan Areas of the United Methodist Church; the Reverend George Grettenberger, Chairperson, Board of Global Ministries of the West Michigan Conference; and the Reverend Gordon Nusz, Chairperson, Board of Global Ministries of the Detroit Conference.

Appendix E
Haïti–Florida Covenant

Covenant Relationship Between The Methodist Church of Haïti and The Florida Conference of The United Methodist Church

In response to the Holy Spirit's call to be united, knit together in Christ and in recognition of the Holy Spirit's power to equip and enable Church Communities to be in mission and ministry together, we join in partnership for Christ, the people of The Methodist Church of Haïti and the people of the Florida Conference of The United Methodist Church. Through this Covenant Relationship, we join together our gifts and graces in a shared vision of ministry.

The historic relationship between The Methodist Church of Haïti and The Florida Conference of The United Methodist Church is enriched by United Methodist lay- and clergypersons of Haïtian descent serving in congregations in Florida and by The United Methodist Volunteers-in-Mission (UMVIM) work teams that have helped to build, rebuild and repair churches, schools and homes in Haïti.

In prayerful consideration of God's will for our churches, we covenant together for the following purposes:

- To develop relationship, mutual understanding, friendship and connections.

- To share cultures, gifts and graces as well as experiences, concerns and hopes.

- To be coordinated and focused in our ministries based on principles of solidarity and love.

- To have regularized standards for ministries.

- To create a method of discerning assets to be shared.

- To actively promote the sharing of resources.

- To share mutual witness to the Christian faith through outreach, teaching and worship.

The first step in giving life to this Covenant is to establish relationships and connections between clergy and laity of The Methodist Church of Haïti and of the Florida Conference of The United Methodist Church. We pledge to make sincere efforts to invite and welcome, to work and worship together, to pray for one another, to attend conferences and educational events together. We will make every effort to share our cultures, to explain our traditions to the best of our abilities and to listen and respect one another.

The cooperative projects and programs in which we enter will be those initiated by The Methodist Church of Haïti and the Florida Conference of The United Methodist Church in accord with the General Board of Global Ministries (GBGM) and UMVIM. No project or program will be initiated without the approval of the President of The Methodist Church of Haïti and of the resident bishop of the Florida Conference of The United Methodist Church.

The sending of work teams from the Florida Conference of The United Methodist Church to Haïti will be coordinated through the UMVIM director in Haïti and

The Florida Conference UMVIM Committee. The financial arrangements will be channeled through recognized means of accountability. When feasible, funds will be channeled through the General Board of Global Ministries. Congregations in the Florida Conference of The United Methodist Church will be requested to remit funds through the Florida Conference treasurer.

There will be two Task Teams established, one by The Methodist Church of Haïti and one by the Florida Conference of The United Methodist Church for the purpose of discerning assets to be shared, needs to be addressed and evaluation of continued ministry together. The Task Teams will actively encourage missionary support through the GBGM for those serving in Haïti and those serving in Florida. They will communicate with each other regularly by e-mail. It is hoped that visitation teams of the Task Teams will meet occasionally and itinerate throughout both connections to interpret the work and cultivate support.

It is agreed that all clergy members of The Methodist Church of Haïti and of the Florida Conference of The United Methodist Church who might be sent to Haïti or to Florida shall do so only through negotiation between the president of The Methodist Church of Haïti and the resident bishop of the Florida Conference of The United Methodist Church in consultation with the General Board of Global Ministries. In any case, no such clergyperson shall function as a resident minister in The Methodist Church of Haïti or in The Florida Conference of The United Methodist Church without prior agreement between The president of The Methodist Church of Haïti and the resident bishop of the Florida Conference of The United Methodist Church through their respective structures. The two church communities are responsible to grant or approve credentials for their respective members. In the case of a visiting pastor, the receiving Church shall acknowledge the pastor's credential as indicated by the sending Church.

We give thanks to God for this shared spiritual journey.

The Rev. Raphael Dessieu,
President of The Methodist Church in Haïti

Bishop Timothy W. Whitaker,
Resident Bishop of the Florida Conference of
The United Methodist Church
Lakeland, June 2006

Appendix F
The Institute of Preaching

Michael Wacht
Lakeland

Some members and pastors of The Methodist Church of Haïti believed the Methodist Church was an isolated church in Haïti, according to the Rev. Dr. Jacques Pierre.

"A villager in Haïti knows about the Methodist church in his area," Pierre said. "He knows about The Methodist Church in Haïti and . . . in the Caribbean. They have not been taught the history of Methodism or how Methodism is a worldwide movement."

This belief has begun to change in part because of efforts by members of the Florida Conference who sponsored and participated in the Institute of Preaching in Haïti. The Institute was held in two sessions, one in March and the other in April, in two different areas of Haïti.

"By receiving funds and guests to help them and be in ministry with them, they had a taste of that connection in a tangible way," Pierre said. "They are part of a much larger Christian movement . . . who are in ministry with them and connected to them through this ministry in Christ's name."

The Institute of Preaching is an annual event in the Florida Conference. It is funded by an endowment given by Mr. and Mrs. Frank Sherman, United Methodists from Florida who believed in "good biblical preaching," according to the Rev. Dr. Gene Zimmerman, a retired pastor and chairman of the Institute of Preaching committee.

The Shermans's original gift of $350,000 was invested and has increased in value, which has allowed the committee to begin exporting the Institute, according to Zimmerman. Nearly 10 years ago, the Florida Conference started offering scholarships to its own institute to pastors from the Methodist Churches in the Bahamas. Three years ago, Florida gave $8,000 to the Methodist Church of Cuba to go toward a Spanish-language Institute for more than 135 pastors and their spouses.

"The first [Cuban] Institute was the first time the ministers and their wives were together at a retreat," Zimmerman said. "It's something they can't afford."

The Haïtian Methodists also requested $8,000 to cover transportation and meals for pastors and travel costs for teachers.

Among the teachers were four Florida Conference pastors, including Pierre and the Revs. Linda Standifer, Luc Dessieux and Montreüil Milord. Dessieux and Milord helped with workshops and worship. Pierre focused on divine grace and human response from a Wesleyan tradition, and Standifer taught pastoral care.

"Pastoral care is a pressing need," Pierre said. "Most of the pastoral duties are performed by lay pastors who have no theological training. They are not only burying the dead but helping the family cope with grief. Receiving training . . . was very valuable to them."

Another aspect of the training was how to do ministry in the Haïtian context. "Theological activities don't take place in a vacuum," Pierre said. "They take place in the context of the reality people are facing every day."

The reality of the Haïtian people is political instability, uncertainty, a lack of safety and employment and inadequate schools and universities, Pierre said. Haïti has mandatory and free education through high school, but the government does not have the resources to provide schools. The private sector is taking over education, but many people cannot afford to send their children to a private school.

"This is why education is an integral part of The Methodist Church in Haïti," he said. Churches offer schooling with low tuition costs to the people in their area. "But when people can't afford the tuition, the churches still provide education," Pierre said. "Ministry and social justice go hand in hand in the Methodist Church of Haïti. Without both, The Methodist Church of Haïti would not be relevant to the suffering and need of the people of Haïti."

Appendix G
Groups Begin Preliminary Work for Long-term Recovery in Haïti

Jenna De Marco
Excerpted from Florida Conference E-review, June 3, 2010

A massive earthquake that shattered Haïti's structural foundations also left behind human emotional, spiritual and physical aftershocks.

Healing that aftermath has become the focus for many in the Florida Conference who want to reach out to the country through established as well as unexpected ministries.

After traveling to Haïti recently the Rev. Beth Fogle-Miller is encouraging a coordinated, long-term response to the unspeakable devastation.

It really is just pretty much beyond description," said Fogle-Miller, who serves as director of Florida Conference Connectional Ministries.

During her trip, Fogle-Miller met with the Rev. Gesner Paul, president of The Methodist Church of Haïti, which has shared in mutual ministry with the Florida Conference for many years, but formally since 2006 when leaders of both churches signed the Haïti/Florida Covenant. Fogle-Miller also met with representatives from United Methodist Volunteers-in-Mission (UMVIM) and United Methodist Committee on Relief (UMCOR).

All the meetings pointed to a desire for better coordination and communication between the conference and these groups so efforts aren't duplicated, she said.

Also, instead of speculating about what help is needed, Fogle-Miller said, it is important to focus on needs The Methodist Church of Haïti has identified. Those include rebuilding schools, churches and homes as well as general redevelopment. Getting schools functioning again is an "essential link in making sure children eat," Fogle-Miller added.

A steering team of people from the Haïti–Florida Covenant task team, the Haïtian ministry team and others familiar with UMCOR and UMVIM processes is being developed, Fogle-Miller said. Pam Garrison, manager of the Florida Conference Disaster Recovery Ministry, will lead the group. The goal is to provide comprehensive information about what various groups are doing and how churches can become involved.

"The conference involvement is not to control it, but rather to facilitate more effective involvement," Fogle-Miller said. "We've also pledged to keep The Methodist Church in Haïti informed as best we can about groups (visiting Haïti) and projects."

Continued prayers are one place churches can begin now to address the "mammoth" needs that resulted from the disaster, Fogle-Miller said. Another "desperate" need, she added, is financial donations to help The Methodist Church of Haïti recover from damage to local churches.

"We took a big financial gift over because they need the money for pastoral salaries and . . . building supplies and labor," Fogle-Miller said. The contribution, totaling $125,000, was collected through Florida Conference Advance Special #100190.

Churches build on relationships

A common, positive thread Fogle-Miller sees in many churches and ministries is their desire not to turn their backs on Haïti in this crisis.

"There was no way you could look at that destruction and then just go on," Fogle-Miller said. "We need to be careful that we respond appropriately and not let it go in the background."

Results of a recent conference survey of churches and outreach ministries show that hundreds of lay and clergy volunteers have already served thousands of hours to aid Haïti's recovery—preparing UMCOR-sanctioned health and layette kits, holding fundraising events, planning for future ventures and providing legal aid.

Several United Methodist church leaders plan to keep the country front and center by continuing or strengthening partnerships established before the earthquake.

At First United Methodist Church in Coral Springs, lay members like mission director Cheryl Price have been traveling to Haïti on mission trips for several years. "God just placed Haïti in my heart," she said, explaining her ongoing passion for the country.

Her church has sent medical teams and helped a Haïtian school, church and foundation—all of which were destroyed or severely damaged in the earthquake. In response to the disaster, the church sent a large shipping container to Haïti filled with 90,000 pounds of medical supplies and food.

Additionally, the church's Haïtian pastor, the Rev. Syler Raymovil, traveled to Haïti in February to help distribute food and assess needs.

"He fed hundreds of people while he was over in Port-au-Prince," Price said.

Members of the congregation are also exploring long-term rebuilding. Two representatives from the church visited Haïti and purchased property in the earthquake-ravaged city of Léogâne, located just west of Port-au-Prince. The goal is to build housing and eventually a new church, school and medical clinic in that location, Price said.

Another plan is to send a medical and construction team to Haïti in mid-September.

Price hopes the work her church is doing—one person at time—is making a difference, despite a situation that sometimes feels overwhelming.

"Sometimes you feel like it's not really much . . . [but] maybe that's all they needed — the hug or that somebody else cared," Price said.

The Rev. Phil Roughton, senior pastor at Christ Church United Methodist in Ft. Lauderdale, is also hopeful his church can play a role in helping even just a portion of Haïti's most vulnerable population—its children.

Reprinted from e-Review Florida United Methodist News Service (http://www.flumc.info).

Appendix H
Memoir of Haïti

Genie Bank
Past President, Women's Division

When I learned of a Volunteers-in-Mission trip to Haïti in the summer of 2009, I was eager to join. The Detroit Conference has had a covenant relationship with the country of Haïti for years, and the leader of the trip had led many trips to Jeremie, Haïti, with the purpose of building a school and church and refurbishing a health clinic in the area.

On January 1, 2010, 17 of us left the United States and landed in Port-au-Prince, Haïti. (That was the last I saw of Port-au-Prince.) We then flew to Jeremie, which is located on the northeast coast of the country. Since it was my first time in Haïti, I was struck by the number of people—young and old—walking down the roads, some headed to markets with baskets of bananas on their heads. If you wanted to get someplace in Haïti, most likely you walked. Arriving at the Jeremie Airport was the real beginning of an adventure not soon forgotten.

The 12 days prior to the earthquake were filled with painting, cleaning, playing with children and working alongside the Haïtians. And we worshiped. The first Sunday was with hundreds of people in a large church in Jeremie and lasted three hours. The next Sunday we worshiped in the country with those we had worked with during the week. Haïtian Christians live a life of love and of hope.

We received word of the earthquake as we were packing and preparing to fly to Port-au-Prince for our journey home. Since there are no televisions and Internet connection is sporadic, we had no idea of the extent of the damage. At breakfast the next morning, word had filtered to Jeremie, and workers came to the Guest House telling of family members who had been killed or were missing. Their grief became our grief as we wept together. The next ferry from Port-au-Prince was overloaded with Haïtians fleeing Port-au-Prince. The population of the area around Jeremie jumped from 17,000 to 70,000+ in just a few weeks. During our extended days, the hospitality of the Haïtians was still evident, as they cared for us, in spite of their overwhelming sadness.

Reflecting on my experience, I realize the earthquake made the world focus on a part of the world that is desperately impoverished. The people of Haïti were poor, but not in spirit. They were poor when we arrived on January 1, and they were poor when we left on January 18. The only difference was the utter destruction of one part of their country. Despite their struggles, the spirit of the people of Haïti is strong. That spirit remains with me.

Deeper Meaning of the Haïtian Proverbs

> *L'Union fait la force*
> (Unity makes strength)
>
> *Yon sèl nou fèb, ansanm nou fò*
> (Alone we are weak,
> but together we are strong)

1. **Bay piti pa chich.** (Give little isn't stingy.)

   Someone gives according to what he or she has, regardless how small it is. When someone gives very little it does not mean he or she is tightfisted.

2. **Di mèsi jwenn ankò.** (Say thank-you receive again.)

   Someone who expresses gratitude when he or she receives a gift encourages the donor to give him or her something else another time.

3. **Pale mal se lapriyè jouda.** (Bad mouthing is gossiper's prayer.)

   You should not pay attention to gossipers' words because bad mouthing others is like a prayer to them; they will always talk bad about others.

4. **Se sou chen mèg sèlman yo wè pis.** (It's only on skinny dogs they see fleas.)

   People always see the poor's flaws, but overlook those of the rich.

5. **Jou va, jou vyen.** (Days go, days come.)

   What goes around comes around. With patience, one day you will have the upper hand.

6. **Yon jou pou chasè yon jou pou jibye.** (One day for hunters one day for prey.)

   The victim will not always be a victim. One of these days, the tables will turn and the victim will be victorious over the oppressor.

7. **Dèyè mòn gen mòn.** (Behind a mountain there is another mountain.)

   What you see is not always all there is; behind each challenge there could be another one.

8. **Gen pouvwa nan non.** (There is power in names.)

   a. Names are significant and powerful, therefore, calling a name could convey meaning and power.

   b. The one who names a person or something has power over it.

9. **Depi tanbou frape fòk Ayisyen danse.** (Whenever the drum beats, Haïtians have to dance.)

The drum is connected to the Haïtians' souls. Therefore, whenever it beats they have to react to it either obviously or subtly.

10. **Bondye bon; Bondye pi fò.** (God is good; God is more powerful.)

God is benevolent and more powerful than any other god. The second part of this proverb is an acknowledgement that there are other powerful deities in the world, but God, the creator of the universe, is the most powerful.

11. **Bondye gen kè sansib pou pòv yo.** (God is compassionate toward the poor.)

God is not indifferent toward the suffering of the poor. God has compassion for them and is in solidarity with the poor.

12. **Fwi pa tonbe lwen pyebwa.** (Fruit does not fall far from the tree.)

Children inherit their parents' qualities or flaws; they are never free from their parents' influences.

13. **Chase sak natirèl, l'ap tounen ap galope.** (Chasing the natural, it will return galloping.)

You cannot get rid of what is naturally a part of who you are. If you do, it will always come back to you faster than you think.

14. **Lanmò pa gen klaksòn.** (Death does not have warning bell.)

As human beings, we could die at anytime and without warning.

15. **Lanmò pa respekte pèsonn.** (Death respects no one.)

Death does not have prejudice or practice favoritism. All of us, rich or poor, regardless of our status, death will come for us.

16. **Men anpil chay pa lou.** (Many hands make weights light.)

When many people work together they can overcome any challenging situation.

17. **Se nan malè ou konnen ki moun ki zanmi w.** (It is in adversity you know who is your friend.)

When you are in difficulty, only your true friends stand by you. Consequently, it is only in adversity you can really know who is a friend of yours.

18. **Apre lapli gen bon tan.** (After the rain there is sunshine.)

A bad or difficult time is like the weather; it will not last forever. One should not be discouraged when one is going through a difficult time, because better days will come.

About the Authors

The Rev. Dr. Jacques E. Pierre

The Rev. Dr. Jacques E. Pierre, also known as Dr. Jep, was born in Haïti, where he served as a youth leader, an itinerant lay preacher and on the Board of Church's Mission. Dr. Jep worked as the coordinator of the National Education Team in charge of the National Program of Literacy and Civic Education led by The Methodist Church in Haïti. He also worked as an adult education consultant for the Center for Human Resources Development (CDRH).

Dr. Jep worked as a social worker at the Church World Service Miami Office, assisting in the resettlement of Cuban and Haïtian refugees. As an ordained elder, Dr. Jep served United Methodist churches in Lakeland and in Miami, Florida. He also worked on the faculty of Trinity International University, South Florida Campus, as an Adjunct Professor of Theology and Biblical Studies.

The Rev. Dr. Jacques E. Pierre holds a diploma in sociology and mass communication from the French Institute of Haïti, a bachelor's degree in human resources management and elementary education from Trinity International University. He also earned a master's of divinity degree in theology and pastoral ministry from Emory University and a PhD in educational leadership with concentrations in theological studies and education from the Union Institute and University. His areas of research and expertise include: adult education, elementary education, transformative learning, church and society and Wesleyan theology. Dr. Jep is the author of *Toward a Better Understanding of Adult Learning: A Critical Analysis of Adult Transformative Learning* and of *Rafrechi Lakonesans* (*Refreshed Knowledge*). He has also published numerous articles on theology and on education.

Dr. Jep is committed to social justice issues and to ministries promoting ethnic and racial understanding and inclusiveness. He is currently teaching in Miami and serving as the pastor of Christ's Community International Ministries, a new multicultural congregation. Dr. Jep and his wife, the Rev. Pascale Delisma-Pierre, live and serve in Miami, Florida. They have three sons.

Dr. M. René Johnson

Dr. M. René Johnson has taught college-level writing courses at a number of institutions, from community colleges to universities. She earned a master of fine arts in creative writing from the Iowa Writers' Workshop and a PhD in rhetoric and technical communication from Michigan Technological University. Her dissertation focused on American Indian treaties and their use in protecting the environment, a passion of hers since the first Earth Day celebration.

In addition to teaching, Dr. Johnson has worked for a number of causes. She served as a US-2 missionary at the Wesley Foundation at Central Michigan University, where she helped organize chapters of Amnesty International, Bread for the World and the NAACP. She also served as a VISTA Volunteer in Iowa, helping to retain families on their farms during the farm crisis.

Currently, Dr. Johnson is active in United Methodist Women, engaged as an officer in the Saginaw Bay District as well as Assistant Dean for the Detroit Conference School of Christian Mission. She also leads a weekly chapel service at her church. René lives in Midland, Michigan, in her childhood home, along with her daughter, Emma, and their two black cats.